THE TREES STOOD STILL

An Unusual Survivor's Story

Sheina Sachar Gertner

Los Angeles   •   Tel-Aviv   •   Lithuania

This book is dedicated to the 5000 inhabitants of Vabolnik who were murdered by the Nazis and the few who dared to defy the odds, escaped, and lived to tell their stories.

"The Tree Stood Still," by Ilya Gertner. ISBN 978-1-58939-886-3.

Published 2024 by Virtualbookworm.com Publishing Inc., P.O. Box 9949, College Station, TX 77842, US. ©1981, 2006, Ilya Gertner. All rights reserved. No part of this publication may be reproduced, stored in a retrieval system, or transmitted in any form or by any means, electronic, mechanical, recording or otherwise, without the prior written permission of Ilya Gertner.

Manufactured in the United States of America.

Sheina Sachar, 1940, one year before the war

I am a living grave. I escaped ten minutes before the murderers came to kill me. I heard with my own ears the last wishes of my parents, my brothers, and my sisters just before they were taken to be killed in the forest. Their voices are still alive in my ears. "Everyone must try to save his life. He must crawl on hands and knees to our homeland, Israel, and tell the world the great crime that has been committed by people who turned out to be worse than beasts in the jungle."

INTRODUCTION

Journal of Middle States Council for the Social Studies, Volume VII, Nos. 1 & 2, FALL, 1984.

THE TREES STOOD STILL
(A Book Review/Essay)
Dr. Albert Nissman
Rider College, Lawrenceville, New Jersey

Sheina Sachar-Gertner. The Trees Stood Still. Framingham, MA: Holocaust Survivors Publishing Co., 1981, 92 pp., $5.95 paperback. (P.O. Box 3252, Framingham, Mass. 01701.)

The Trees Stood Still is a first-person narrative written by Sheina Sachar Gertner, a Lithuanian-born school teacher, saved ten minutes before her Nazi executioners came to kill her. She now devotes all her time to Holocaust Studies, lecturing in Israel and in the Boston area.

Ms. S-G's narrative, written in present-tense staccato sentences and short stark paragraphs, penetrates with vivid imagery our gateways to the mind: vision; hearing; touch; smell; balance; and human sensibilities. Referring to herself as *"a living grave"* whose anguish and anxiety are still very much alive, whose life is etched by pain of memory, Ms. S-G has dedicated her life to *"tell the world the great crime that has been committed by people who turned out to be worse than beasts in a jungle:'*

Yet, there was a stillness, death in the air. extermination on earth. The tree of Judaism was truncated: its limbs and branches severed; its very seeds destroyed; the crown and flower of Jewry uprooted. Not only did the trees stand still but the world remained mute. Neighbors and friends did not know, did not want to know, and did not care that in

*the midst of their lives the destruction of six million
Jews by fire and gas was in progress. The dark,
treeless, fiery Holocaust raged wildly.*

Ms. S-G's tranquil life was torn asunder and her parents,
brothers, and sisters were murdered in Vabolnik. Lithuania where
her family had lived for more than 100 years. And, I as a reader,
think: "When is a family considered bona fide residents? How
long do Jews have to reside in a nation before they are
established as welcome citizens?" (Not so parenthetically, I
know a Jew that the Nazis uprooted from Frankfurt, Germany
where his family had lived for seven generations – 140 - 210
years. Citizenship is an illusory goal for Jews in most countries
in the world. There is a message here: Jews assimilate at their
own peril; this was true in the 1940's; it is equally true in the
1980's.)

The Holocaust gave birth to rationalization. In some ways,
rationalization is a form of resistance; however, it can also be a
brake on life-saving action. Ms. S-G and her family devise
"elaborate ways to explain our survival to ourselves." The
Nazis, they rationalized, would not kill the Jews for many good
(vs. real) reasons: the Nazis could benefit from the Jews' labor;
strong, healthy people will not be killed; revenge will not be
taken on all Jews; not all Jews are Communists; *"Lithuanians
are Christians, doesn't their God forbid killing?"* Other
rationalizations abound. An old religious Jew opines, *"If it is the
will of our God, we cannot change anything."*

The tears, the doubts, the hopes co-mingle. Optimism and
pessimism ride emotional see-saws. Love and hate ride the waves
of feelings. The reader relives the anguish.

A Jew on his knees is whipped by a Nazi. *"No brain
can imagine the devil who murders children."* People try to
escape. Some are paralyzed by inaction born of hope, of fear, of
doubt. Disaster looms large. The reader relives the anguish.

The ancient Hebrew watchword of the Jewish people is
sounded.

"Shema Israel–Hear, O Israel, the Lord of our God, the Lord is One...." reverberates as the trees stand still.

The reader relives the anguish.

> *I look through the cracks between the boards of the stable. Nobody is outside. Again I talk to my God. 'Here is our end. Are we, Jews, worse than the others? What crimes have we committed? God! Why do you not protect us? I am so miserable. Oh God! I beg you for mercy. This is the end. We will not survive. This is the end of the Jews. No one will know.*

And, the reader relives the anguish.

Ms. S-G thinks of her Christian friends and neighbors who have forsaken her and her fellow Jews. There is a litany of searing questions and statements.

> *Jesus, why can you not cut the hands of the murderers? Why do you not help them to defeat their beastly instincts? The murderers go to church and bless your name. They have faith in you. They have promised you to be noble. On Sundays they go to church in their best clothes. Now, I see two neighbors who eagerly obey the command to kill. Where are you Jesus?*

And, the reader relives the anguish.

Of Hitler and the human race, there is another litany:

> *Hitler is the mightiest power in Europe. Why did he choose to do battle with Jewish children? He may be crazed or mad, but why does he have so many followers? Do they still feel like other humans? I want to shout, to hit my head against the wall. Suddenly, through the cracks I see a cat. It stands calmly and wiggles its tail. It is very quiet. I press both my hands onto my lips and try to swallow a stream of tears.*

And, the reader relives the anguish.

Vignettes of country life in Lithuania pepper this slim volume: thunder; waiting for miracles; peasants providing food to homeless Jews; some few Christian peasant farmers, at the risk of their own lives, hiding and feeding Jews; Jews wandering in unbearable cold and dense darkness, speaking in low voices; Jews hiding like fugitives; shedding tears over guilt for leaving family behind; Nazis barking to Jews: "Take off your clothes. Run to your graves now!"

And, the reader relives the anguish.
The fugitive life, this scraping for survival take its toll.

... Chaim [Sheina's husband] and I become different human beings, without emotions, without feelings. We do not smile; we do not cry. We talk very little. Every morning we face the mere fact that we must have survived only to wake up one more morning. In the evenings we talk about the past, about the present. We have no future.

Dehumanization, courtesy of the Nazis, is writ large!

And, the reader relives the anguish.

There is a portrait of Sheina Sachar (p. 2), circa 1938, one year before the war. She is a beautiful young woman. I was haunted by her intense beauty. I was torn by the thought that six million Sheina's and Chaim's - six million Jews were destroyed for one "reason" – they were Jews!

Other pictures follow. A few episodes in lives and lifestyles that are no more. The pictures enhance the narrative. But the tragedy of the Holocaust is just too immense to be totally captured. Sheina's words and pictures, however, do "freeze" some of the essence of what was - and what might have been.

The reader must overlook some of the uneven writing. He must forgive some typos, the contradiction between the preface and the dedication, between the table of contents and some of the chapter headings. But this is all minutia. The real thing – and it is very real – is the total impact of the book!

I recommend this book for all teachers and their students from grades seven through twelve and beyond. We have an obligation to awaken from our slumber the humanity that has been sedated by apathy and ignorance. The Trees Stood Still can help wake us up.

No review of Holocaust memoirs can evoke the horror and anxiety. Only a careful reading can get us to see and feel some fragments of the Holocaust. A careful reading helps us to feel that universal cry in the author's down-to-earth call, *"I do not want to be killed. The desire to live is strong."* A longing is born when Sheina and Chaim come upon their former family homestead in their wanderings from farm to farm.

> *Forever! Nobody wants us. Not even my childhood friend Adzia came and offered us shelter. We have been driven out of our house. Somebody is using our house without being punished. Somebody is using our furniture. It is not a crime to steal property from the Jews.*

There are serious implications for educators and education:

> *What a wonderful world has been created for the wild beasts. I am not afraid of the beasts although Tamulionis warned me about the wolves in the forest. Among them I can breathe freely. I am afraid, however, of men.*

> *I decide neither to weep nor to think of death. Among my herd and flock I begin to think of my days at school. I*

accuse my teachers. They taught me to be religious, to love physical work. Nobody taught me how to protect myself against an attack by a nazi.

Sheina Sachar-Gertner, as survivor, feels guilt and gladness that she is alive. But she has the albatross of obligation forever around her neck. She must question Jews, Christians, Nazis and God. Her questions are not academic questions from philosophy and theology. They are questions forged from the sinews of her personhood.

At times. Ms. S-G ruminates as her own persecutor–accuser. *"You could have been more useful in family, in society. You have missed a lot of opportunities."* Perhaps, she has. But as educators in a democratic republic, we have no reason to miss opportunities. This book is her testament, her instrument of catharsis, her way of shedding her albatross.

In the past, the world stood still – mute, unmoved, uncaring. If we as teachers do likewise, what will our testament be? What will our catharsis be, how shall we shed our albatross?

Biographical Notes: Dr. Albert Nissman is Professor of Education in the Division of Graduate Studies, Rider College, and is Co-Editor of this Journal.

MARTYRDOM AND RESISTANCE

Jan.-Feb. 1984 - Shevat-Adar 15744

The Trees Stood Still. Sheina Sachar-Gertner
Holocaust Survivors Publishing Co.

Reviewed by DR. MARK W. WEISSTUCH

In 1941, Sheina Sachar-Gertner was a young newly married school teacher in a small Lithuanian town. When the Germans invaded, she and her husband, Chaim, made the fateful decision to seek refuge in the countryside. Her parents and the rest of her family remained. Moments after their departure, all the Jewish inhabitants of the town were brutally rounded-up, carted to the outskirts of the town and murdered.

Sheina and her husband spent the rest of the war wandering from farm to farm dressed as beggars, *"without feelings, without hopes, without fears."* They hid in hovels and barns, hounded by informers and pursued by fierce Lithuanian Nazis. For food and shelter they depended on the grudging beneficence of surly peasants, some of whom had been "friends" of her family before the war.

Sheina (and Chaim) survived, and The Trees Stood Still chronicles the story of her survival. But this slim, muted memoir is also an effort at expiation. For Sheina, her flight, as the Nazis were loading their guns, is tantamount to an act of abandonment and betrayal which has left her permanently scarred. When two spinster sisters, righteous gentiles, who provide the desperate refugees with their first shelter, impart the grim, harrowing details of the mass slaughter in the forest, Sheina is stunned. Her deepest fears are confirmed. Her entire existence thereafter is riveted to this one event: "Every morning we face the mere fact that we must have survived only to wake up one more morning. In the evenings we talk about the past, about the present. We have no future."

THE WILL TO LIVE

Guilt haunts her constantly and intensifies as her fortunes improve. However, it does not mitigate her will to live nor does it attenuate her deeply religious beliefs. Before the war, her faith in God served as the ethical basis of her life. As she witnesses and experiences the callous inhumanity of a world driven by madness and apparent godlessness, she grapples with her faith. *Is this God's test of the honest people?* she wonders. She questions and accuses God, but she never doubts or rejects His presence. In the face of the murderers' rampage, God assumed a remote, stony silence. In the forest on that baleful day, *"The inhuman shout, the cries of women and children did not reach the heavens."* Nature, too, was silent, indifferent, helpless, as the image of the book's title suggests, in the midst of so much human suffering. Yet, Sheina comes to an accommodation with God. She begins to understand, while she is shepherdess to a flock of sheep, that God is incapable of intervening in the affairs of men just as he cannot prevent the lion from devouring its victim.

EXPERIENCES AFTER WAR

The question which lurks behind every step Sheina takes toward her survival and safety is *"Why me?"* - why was I chosen to survive when all the others were killed? This survivor's account does not end with the liberation, but continues on into the post-war years as the author re-establishes her teaching career and raises a family of her own. Annually, she brings her children on of pilgrimage to the graves in the forest. Years later, despite the opposition of the Soviet government, she is instrumental in erecting a commemorative monument at the site of the massacre. Rather than allaying her onus, these efforts sharpen her remorse: *"I shall never forget you. Now we have a monument. Still, I am guilty for escaping, my dear mother and father ... I don't even know when your hearts stopped. I pray in my heart to God to punish me."* The struggle to survive persists long after the Nazis were vanquished. The enemy becomes memories and the tears they prompt.

Biographical Notes: Dr. Weisatuch is the administrator of Temple Shalom, Newton, Massachusetts.

JUDAICA BOOK NEWS,
Fall/Winter 1983/4, 5744, Volume 14, Number 1

COURAGEOUS AND MOVING

Unlike the stories of children who survived the war by hiding among the peasants, The Trees Stood Still reveals the experiences of a sensitive, insightful woman. Sheina Sachar-Gertner distills her thoughts and feelings in a compellingly personal, courageous and moving book. Its terse, compressed style evokes the sense of a confessional. What emerges, despite the pain, is an affirmation of mankind's humanity from an individual who is strongly committed to life at the same time that she is forever attached to the souls of the dead. At the end of the book, Sheina, finally granted her emigration papers by the Russians, and she is on the plane headed toward Israel. Clutching two-red-tulips in her hand, she thinks, *"I cannot forget. All I can do is hope."*

Though it was not written with this intent, The Trees Stood Still, because of its positive outlook and because it is sparing and understated in its description of violence, could serve as an introductory reading about the Holocaust for adolescents. Its delineations of the complexities and questions inherent in the afterlife of survivors is also most valuable in this regard.

SHEINA SACHAR-GERTNER was born in Vabolnik, a small town in Lithuania where her ancestors had lived for hundreds of years. Sheina left Vabolnik and graduated from the Teachers' College in Memel. She started her first teaching job, got married but World War II erupted. She did not live in camps and ghettoes; she did not see a single German; she did not see a murdered body -- but she lived each day fearing death. She escaped with her husband just before they were taken to the graves.

After the war, she taught at a Lithuanian school in Kovno. Sheina participated in the first hunger strike in front of the Kremlin in search for her final exit visa to Israel. Just twenty-five years after the war she was allowed to emigrate. Today her free time is dedicated to Holocaust studies. She continues to lecture in Israel and in the Boston area.

In memory of
my parents and my youngest brother,
Berale

ONE.

THE WAR

It is June 1941. The school year has just ended. Chaim and I take one suitcase and go to visit my parents in Vabolnik. We also plan to spend a week at Palanga, the sea resort. We do not even take our monthly wages for the summer vacation because we hope to be back in two weeks. I bring books and magazines to read which I know cannot be found in Vabolnik.

I have presents for nearly every member of my family. I intended to buy a hat for my father, but, not finding the right size, I postponed it for a later date. My father never got the hat.

On June 20, we arrive at my parent's house in Vabolnik. As I read magazines full of articles about the war in Europe, I hope it will not affect us immediately. There is no fear of war in Vabolnik. My mother prepares potato dumplings, my favorite childhood dish, and everybody here seems to be occupied by day-to-day activities. Life is normal in the neighborhood.

On the second day, however, we hear explosions of bombs in the air, far away from our town. We are shocked. The war! We are still confident in the strength of the Russian Army. On the radio we hear the news announcements regarding the new laws directed against the Jews. Incredible! Nobody believes the news.

Through the window we watch the street. It is in chaos. We see Jews with suitcases and bags rushing out of their houses. A neighbor drops by to borrow rope to tie his bundle. He is walking to the train station in Subatch, twenty-five miles away. His aim - to reach the eastern border of Russia.

Most of the Jewish population decides to leave Vabolnik and move closer to the Russian border. But how? There are no buses. Nobody has a car.

A few lucky ones have horses and carts; many others use baby carriages to wheel their possessions. Everyone drags his belongings to the train station.

My father and three brothers want to stay home because my father is sick. He is not afraid of the Germans. The German soldiers have stayed in his house during World War I, they even shared food with his family. Still, Chaim and I decide to go to the train station.

While my youngest brother Berale gets the horse ready for the cart, I look out the front window of our house. I see a parade of sad, worried faces passing by. All the Jews are in a hurry as if they were told the town is going to be bombed. Across the street a Lithuanian neighbor, not a Jew, is taking out a pail of water. His face is calm. He does not even glance at the troubled crowd across the street.

When we leave the town we see only two carts filled with people. Several dozen families are walking. Everyone carries a satchel in his hand.

Our plan is to get back to our apartment, to take a few belongings and then move towards the Russian border. On the way to the train station we are quiet. Chaim worries- "What will we do if there is no train?" I do not answer. I think. I see myself in Russia. Will the Germans allow the Jews who stayed behind to receive letters and parcels from Russia? When will we be able to meet again?

A few hours later we arrive at the station. The only train in the station is overcrowded. Nobody knows what is happening; where the train is heading. Still, Chaim and I jump on the train. Berale stays on the platform. But, the moment the train starts moving I jump from it. I hear myself murmuring "I do not want to leave alone." Chaim follows.

We are back home that same evening. Again we are quiet. Everyone waits to see what tomorrow will bring.

The next day many people who went West, and not to the train station, return. They all met German soldiers. Only one man, Toker, did not come back. He hanged himself. He left a note that read "Better to die by my own hands than by the hands of the Germans."

Maybe Toker was a clever man, I thought. But I could not believe life would not soon return to normal. After all, wars end.

On the fourth night after the war started the Lithuanian Nazis begin their movement against us. They boast with satisfaction-"The time has come for revenge on the Jews. The Jews are communist collaborators." The next day they arrest twenty. (Much later we learn that they were killed in Kupishky.) Among these victims is Chaim Kruk, a Zionist all his life. This association does not help. Chaim Kruk is arrested with a group of communists. He keeps repeating, "It's a mistake, I am not a communist... Nothing helps. He is shot with the communists.

Young Lithuanian men come to every Jewish house and give orders. The Jews are put to work at their orders. The work consists of sweeping the market place, washing the floors of offices or cleaning Lithuanian shops.

The first few days my mother works instead of me. I stay home. She fears for me. Being very young, just out of college, I may lose my temper. A few days later I insist I should go in her place.

My first job is to sweep the floors of the local police station. The chief police officer sits at a table and scribbles on a piece of paper. From time to time he catches a glimpse of me. He knows me well; he is our neighbor. Before the war, he was an employee at a little grocery shop. His eyes are always full of joy. Now, he has the power to force a teacher, a bright student, to obey his orders. I get irritated. Blood rises to my head. I feel like smashing something against his head. "Let's not tease the animal," I think this time. Does that make me weak?

3

In a short time our lives were overturned. In the country, the Jews lived in peace and friendship with their neighbors for hundreds of years. There were Hebrew high schools in the bigger towns, grade schools in all little towns; there were "Yeshivot." I attended a religious Hebrew school called "Yavne." I attended Zionist clubs where we danced the "hora." For a time it seemed that the Jewish culture was blossoming. Now, suddenly, everything has changed.

The Nazis prepare our thoughts for the nearest future. They tell us that in a few weeks we are going to be sent to labor-camps where we will stay until the end of the war. In the meantime, they force us to leave our houses and move to Paris Street where formerly only Lithuanians lived.

Every Lithuanian wants a big Jewish house. And he gets it. We go to Paris Street to search for a two-room house in exchange for our six-room house. The owners speak kindly. They assure us that after the war they will return our house.

We do not trust them. Again, we borrow a horse and a cart, pack our most valuable furniture and take it to a farmer, a friend of my parents, in a nearby village. We do hope to reclaim it after the war. He invites Chaim, my brother and me to stay with him for a few days. We accept his invitation.

Three days later, two Nazis arrive in a truck. They order us to get on it. "Hurry!" they shout. One of them hits me with his left hand and with both hands fiercely pulls off my gold ring. I know him! His family lives near our town. Every Sunday the family used to come to church in our town and leave their cart in our yard. They were friends of my parents.

I am shocked. I cannot calm myself down. But I do not cry. In twenty minutes they bring us back home to my parents' house. My mother and father look sad. They look up but say nothing. That makes me angry. I tell them, "We have to go to the country. We have to find a real friend. We must hide. "Where?" asks my father.

A few days ago an old friend, Stuckas, came to our house. He simply walked into the house, chose a few of my father's suits, a pair of shoes, a watch and left. He did it in the presence of the whole family. No longer is it a crime to rob a Jew.

In the evening we discuss our situation. I keep talking about resisting, about setting, houses on fire, about revenge. The older ones threaten me- "You are going to kill us all. Don't you dare!"

The tension among us is numbing. We try to go to sleep. But I cannot stay in bed. I see my mother in her bed, I hear her sighing the whole night. "Mother," I think, "I too am afraid that the Nazis will come tonight."

I pull Chaim close to me. We hold each other as if to keep us from departing from this world forever. We do not sigh.

We hardly breathe.

The morning of August 20, 1941 we get new orders. We must prepare food for three days and go to the Synagogue. We obey. The Nazis, already there, intercept us and check our bags. They grab Chaim's hand and take off his ring. Then they snatch my gold chain. They order us to climb up onto one of the two trucks that will take us to a bigger town Posvol, twenty-five miles away. The trucks are too small and cannot hold all the people at once. Chaim and I are left behind. We spend another night on the floor of the Synagogue. We talk of escaping. "Where?" Chaim asks, as my father had done before.

In the morning we find out that the two Vainer brothers have escaped.

It is already late in the morning when a driver and an armed nazi arrive in a truck. We are told to get on it, pack together, step on one another if we must, but squeeze in tight, like cattle. My parents and my two brothers were already taken away in a truck yesterday. Now Chaim, my youngest brother and I wait and wait. We try to be the last ones in the line.

Nobody talks. Everyone in the Synagogue yard is nervously pacing, waiting for his turn. I am repeating prayers from the Sidur, which I remember. To every prayer I add my own sentences- "Oh God, do help us to overcome any disaster that is awaiting us." I am very suspicious. I talk aloud. "They are going to kill us." But nobody listens to me.

There is some hope that they are going to take us to a labor camp. Death frightens me terribly. I do not think about the wish to live. In my heart I decide to wait until the last moment and then jump into the well. I am preoccupied only with myself.

From the corner of the Synagogue yard I can see the Market Square. It is Tuesday. Farmers from surrounding villages are in the market to buy various necessities. Suddenly I notice two local people in the crowd. They are selling our pillows, sheets, and clothes -- the belongings we had left behind in our house. A large crowd of farmers -- hungry dogs -- pushing each other, fighting to obtain a better deal. "It's a disaster. They will kill us"- I shout. An old man turns slowly to me, "Relax, we have time"- he says. "We will buy new things. We have time."

Suddenly, too fast, our turn comes. We get onto the truck. The driver turns to the right, the road that leads from Vabolnik to Posvol. On the way we pass some peasants on foot. They stop and look at us. The truck stops in one yard to get some water. There are about ten people working. Their faces seem to be confused, maybe ashamed. One woman rubs her eyes with her sleeve.

TWO.

POSVOL

Whon we arrive at Posvol I am more relaxed. I begin to believe the story about labor camps. The truck brings us to the gates of the street where the Jews are concentrated. We get off and face two armed young men standing guard. They order us to the school.

Chaim, I and the other thirty-five people from Vabolnik enter the school. In the school there are a few vacant rooms. We settle in one corner and start searching for my parents.

We walk along the street asking where the Jews from Vabolnik are. Somebody points us to our right. There I see my parents and the rest of my family sitting in the yard. They are sad, their worried faces show fear. "Heavens knows what will happen," are my mother's first words. "Don't panic!" my father assures us, "We will see."

My parents and two brothers had arrived yesterday, and found a very small room. Chaim and I spend the whole day with them. In the evening we must leave them and return to the school. There the floor is our bed; our clothes are our mattresses.

During the day we walk around the town and discuss our situation. What should we do? We live like poor immigrants. We know the exact amount of our food ration. We count pieces of bread. We are promised new food supplies at the end of the week.

It surprises me, but we do get adjusted to our camp life. Many people sew satchels and cotton bags to make the packing easier. The whole time is spent mostly packing; very little of it is spent talking.

Chaim and I visit our neighbor, Benjamin. He is calm and we discuss our options in the labor camp. "The guards are really nice to us," says Benjamin. "They are not cruel. We are free to walk. They are not afraid that we will escape." (We have no place to escape, I think.) "We must wait and hope for the best," concludes Benjamin. Chaim echoes this acceptance, "We have to see what the local Jews are going to do. They know some of the guards." Chaim spends the whole day in discussions on the subject of camps and guards. The sentence "We will see, maybe tomorrow," ends each conversation."

As the evidence of the approaching tragedy accumulates, we construct more and more elaborate ways to explain our survival to ourselves. The Nazis can benefit from our work. Not all the Jews are communists. Why should they take revenge on all of us? Why should they kill young, strong, and healthy people? Lithuanians are Christians, doesn't their God forbid killing?

Arlik, a very old religious man, puts on his glasses and says in a calm voice: "If it is the will of our God, we cannot change anything."

"If we don't do anything, even the angels won't help us," says Benjamin Slavin. He is a younger man, about thirty-five. Though he seems to be more aggressive, even his advice is only caution and patience. "Let's wait until tomorrow," concludes Benjamin.

Some of us, especially the younger women, again start talking about acting, putting houses on fire. What else can we do? Among us there are many strong, healthy, and intelligent people. However, the elders advise caution, obedience and nobody dares to disobey them.

I persist on trying to convince my parents--"We have to run!"

I see tears in my father's eyes. I torture him with schemes to find a place to hide. "Where will we go? Who will take care of us?" my father keeps repeating. "Don't you remember our friend Stuckas who robbed us in the middle of the day, in our presence. Nobody will protect us!" He says no more. His eyes are sad and disappointed. He bites his lips and looks at us bitterly.

Chaim becomes pessimistic. "We have no place to go. Maybe we will find an opportunity tomorrow."

To be ready for any situation, everyone dresses in many layers: three shirts, two trousers, and several jackets one on top of the other. Contradictory thoughts obsess our minds: How can we survive? Can we escape? How will the murderers commit their crime? Will they come with knives, as the Ukranians did forty years ago during the pogroms? What should we do when they come? Jump into the well at the horrible moment. On the contrary, argue others, everyone has to think how to remain alive. We do not cry, we just argue. We are depressed.

August 26. I remember this day locked like a crystal in my mind. Our discussion ended at nine o'clock in the morning when my mother came to our place at the school. Her cheeks were red with fear: "Buses came into our street"- she whispered- "The buses are packed with armed young fellows: Lithuanians, Latvians, and Ukrainians. Today they take us to the camps. Please, hurry, come with Chaim and have a good breakfast before the journey." She left.

Chaim shaves in a hurry. He packs a few heavy sweaters for my parents. Then we run to Paris Street. My mother has disappeared in the mournful crowd. The policeman stops Chaim and me. He does not let us enter the street, and directs us back to wait for the buses to arrive. I never saw my mother again.

We return to the school building. From the balcony I can clearly see what is happening in the street. I see the crowd armed with guns and whips. They enter the houses of the Jews. They kick the Jews out of their homes. A few young fellows try to resist but the sticks of the murderers quickly subdue them. An old Jew falls on his knees before a nazi. He murmurs something. His murmurs are answered by the whip slashing to the right and to the left. The old one gets up, takes his bag, his suitcase, and hurries to the bus.

Suddenly, on the West Side of our street I spot the Kirshon family. Mr. Kirshon, his wife and two children dressed in winter clothes have crossed the street to the non-Jewish section. It is a Lithuanian street! Is somebody trying to save their lives? For money? Or is it a friend?

Kirshon heads a respected family in Posvol. He is a lawyer, a former teacher. He has worked in a Lithuanian school before the war. Is a good friend saving them?

Chaim and I return to the room where the rest of us from Vabolnik gather. Nobody knows if and how the Kirshon family succeeded in their attempt to escape. I try to talk with Chaim Ziv.

Chaim Ziv is a clever, respectable man. He is a newcomer to our town. Still, in only a few years, he has succeeded in reconstructing an old building that stood abandoned for many years. He managed to erect a factory for spinning wool and another one for weaving. In addition, Chaim built a power plant. He is an authority, a powerful man.

Chaim Ziv is sad. In a low voice he repeats several times, "No brain can imagine the devil who murders children." Finally he adds, "If ... if ... anybody stays alive, he must tell the world."

The fear grows. Disaster is getting nearer.

Still, the decision is to wait. People keep repeating, "Wait, wait... If somebody saves his life, he should tell the world of the crimes." "Nobody will believe! Murderers have all the power," says Benjamin raising his fists over his head.

THREE.

ESCAPE

Suddenly, the door opens. An old priest comes into our room. Sad and frightened, he whispers, "My friends, don't believe the Nazis. They are not taking you to the camps. They will take you to the forest. They will take you to Abraham." With horror as if bitten by a snake, we all run to the yard.

Chaim and I run to the guard Aleksas. Since I had studied with his wife in college, this kind of a friendship, I thought, might make him softer. I give him my ring and a handbag. I ask him not to look toward the fence.

We jump over the fence. We do not speak. We do not cry. Everyone is frightened. Everyone runs in a different direction.

Chaim and I run to the right. We turn left. We stop running. I feel like a lamb attacked by a wolf. I do not think. I only repeat, "Shema Israel, Shema... Are they going to kill us? Oh God, where are you? Where?"

I am waiting for a bullet to hit me any moment. I glance back and see Chaim following.

Suddenly, I hear shots fired. I stop and close my eyes. "Shema Israel, Adonoi..." I shiver. I open my eyes. I am still alive. Frightened, I move forward. Looking for a shadow to hide. Again, another shot.

My left hand touches a wooden wall. My right hand opens a broken door. Chaim follows. The door closes by itself. When my eyes get used to darkness I realize we are in a shed for goats. I do not move.

I stand with my back to the door. My hands are clasped together near my lips as if holding my murmuring- "Shema Israel, Shema..." My body is a stone, ready to fall when a bullet sticks in my back. I tremble and open my eyes. Through the cracks on the roof I see a small branch has fallen from a tree.

I am still waiting for a bullet. I do not utter a sound. Death is not fearful to me anymore. All feelings have left me. Minutes pass by, one after another.

I look through the cracks between the boards of the stable. Nobody is outside. Again I talk to my God, "Here is our end. Are we, Jews, worse than the others? What crimes have we committed? God! Why do you not protect us? I am so miserable. Oh God! I beg you for mercy. This is the end. We will not survive. This is the end of the Jews. Nobody will know.

"No dog will bark!"

Chaim and I take a few steps forward. We turn our faces to the door. Nobody has uttered a sound.

Any movement outside touches my heart, "The murderer is coming." I am ready to attack him with nails, but nobody comes. The sun is about to set, and we are standing still.

"We shall not avoid death," says Chaim.

In the stable, the whole time I accuse God. "Oh my God of Abraham. Why don't you pity the little children? There are so many prayers in our Sidur, you are the greatest power in the world, the greatest authority to pity the people, to forgive us for our faults. I have been blessing your sacred name for being so generous to me. Oh God where are you? Oh God!"

I can not speak. I blame myself for leaving my parents. Hiding in the little muddy goat shed, I am like the young Jewish fellows in the poem by Bialik, called "The Slaughter". He described the pogrom in Kishinev when the Jewish youth did not resist. Thirty-six years have passed, and here I am hidden in a hole. Shame! As a teacher, I had been so quick to accuse those Jews. And now? I recite Bialik's poem,

Oh heavens,
Do ask pity and mercy for me.
If you have the God in your heart,
If you know the way to him and
I have not found the way.
So, heavens, you pray for me.
I myself, my heart is dead.
I have no prayers any more.
To revenge little children?
The devil himself
Has not yet created such revenge.

I repeat the poem in my heart. Maybe there is another God who will save babies from the Lion's claws?

I think and see our yard in my little town. I play with Lithuanian children from the neighborhood. My friend, Verute, prays to Jesus every time she loses a game. I ask why she is mentioning her God's name every minute.

"Jesus is the best," she says. "If you get a slap on one cheek, you must turn the other cheek. Jesus helps all the people who have faith in him, who pray for him. Jesus helps people not to commit crimes."

The last thought draws my attention. "Jesus, why can you not cut the hands of the murderers? Why do you not help them to defeat their beastly instincts? The murderers go to church and bless your name. They have faith in you. They have promised you to be noble. On Sundays they go to church in their best clothes. Now, I see two neighbors who eagerly obey the command to kill. Where are you Jesus?"

I pronounce aloud the last word Jesus. Chaim, as if pushed by an invisible force, strongly steps aside. Again he repeats the same sentence: "We will not avoid death. Not one local inhabitant will help us. Where can we go?" he asks me. "How can we hide our frightened faces?" I think.

Hitler is the mightiest power in Europe. Why did he choose to do battle with Jewish children? He may be crazed or mad, but why does he have so many followers? Do they still feel like other humans? I want to shout, to hit my head against the wall. Suddenly, through the cracks I see a cat. It stands calmly and wiggles its tail. It is very quiet. I press both my hands onto my lips and try to swallow a stream of tears.

We stand and wait. The sound of thunder comes from far away. I begin to hope for a miracle.

I begin to believe in the grace of God. Maybe our God has his own ideas. Maybe his will is a test, a trial of the honest people. A test for the beast among the human beings. Inside my heart there still lives a childish faith. A miracle, only a miracle...

The door opens. A woman with a goat steps into the shed. Seeing us, she screams. I pronounce three words: "We are Jews." She leaves the goat in the shed and runs away telling us she will bring us some food. Immediately we leave.

Again we are wandering. We go to the east; to the west. We change our direction several times until we find our way to the bushes, to the darkness, far away from people. It is raining. We are lost.

It suddenly becomes clear- we cannot save our lives without the help of people. We see a man standing near a little house. We ask him for shelter in a stable. He refuses but points towards his neighbor, Cheponis, who is working in the field. We have no choice. We approach Cheponis and ask him for shelter. He hesitates.

Suddenly a young fellow with a gun on his shoulder appears. Cheponis tells us to move aside. They talk for about ten minutes. They speak in low voices as though they are arguing a friendly manner. At last the fellow goes away.

In my heart I believe he is a nazi. Chaim agrees with me. Nothing around me touches my heart. We are in the hands of blind fate. A voice inside repeats, "You could have been murdered but your eyes can still see the fields and the cloudy skies."

Cheponis takes us to his large house, and leaves us alone in a room. We do not even whisper. Maybe in a few minutes someone else will come in and take us to the slaughter place.

I look through the window. A woman carries two buckets. She has just milked the cows. Another woman helps ready the horse to take in the full carriage of straw to the store. Others watch the crops. I think, this is life, going on as usual.

At the same time, murderers are probably killing my mother, frightened children and babies. I cannot yet believe it.

An hour later the farmer with his two sons come into the room. They talk about the horrible times that have fallen upon the Jews, about the Germans who have occupied the country, and about the young Lithuanians who help the Germans. Chaim joins the conversation. I can not speak at all. I am rigid.

The woman sets the table. The table is full with chicken, cheese and butter. Nothing has happened.

I can hardly eat bread and milk. But I go ahead and eat. I try not to sigh. I think, "Forgive me, oh God, for leaving my parents alone, among the beasts in the forest."

Later the farmer takes us into a small room to sleep. Before leaving he tells us, "Tomorrow we will see what we can do."

I collapse onto the bed. The pillow hides my face full of tears. Chaim is quiet. I hear the sound of thunder. A miracle must happen! We are in the hands of fate. At six o'clock in the morning I wake up- still in tears. Is it true? Will the murderers kill even the little children? What will happen to the babies?

The farmer comes and brings along an old woman. She offers us shelter for a few days. She wants to help us for the love of their God. We follow her.

Chaim and Sheina, 1941.

Sheina Sachar-Gertner

With friends in Teachers' College, Memel, 1938.

With classmate in High School, Posvol, 1935.

With classmates in Grade School, Vabolnik, 1928.

Sheina's whole family at her parent's house in Vabolnik, 1941.

Parents in Vabolnik, 1940.

Brother Itzhak in Vabolnik, 1940.

Brother David in Vabolnik, 1940

Teaching in Jewish School in Vilky, 1941.

FOUR.

FIRST SHELTER

Our way is through the bushes to avoid people. It is the beginning of autumn. Farmers are in the fields. Everybody works alone. No groups are to be seen. An hour later we come to a little house. The house has no floors. Earth and sand cover the ground in the house. In another room, we see a woman sweeping the dirt floor with a broom made of small tree branches. She sighs and weeps in silence.

The woman who brought us finally introduces herself- "I am Petronele, and this is my sister, Elizabeth. We have a small house but we will find a place for you." Elizabeth sighs again and begins to weep. The sisters ask us to sit down. They both remain standing. "We are going to help you for the sake of our Christian God," says Petronele. "We regret the evil crimes done to your people," adds Elizabeth. They speak in turn, in a low voice. Then Petronele leaves and Elizabeth goes to the kitchen to prepare breakfast.

One table is in the corner. A wooden bench is against the wall. Another bench is in front of the table and there is one small chair that is all the furniture. In another corner there is a loom filled with woolen threads of four colors. The older sister, Elizabeth, is the weaver.

Elizabeth and Petronele have only one cow that provides them with milk, sour cream and butter; one apple tree and a small vegetable garden in the yard. Elizabeth weaves cloth for the richer neighbors. Petronele, the younger sister, helps the neighbors take in crops. That is their entire income.

Yet, they share with us their last piece of bread, their last apple from the tree. We have no valuables, no money, nothing to pay them with.

They do not ask for our work. Still, I try to help Petronele with sewing. Chaim grinds the grain with an old millstone placed in the little room where we hide during the day. We are not allowed to go outdoors. Nobody must know about us. We have plenty of time to think and to talk. Sometimes I get the feeling that I have moved to another planet.

With plenty of time to think, I remember my life in the past when I was still on earth. All my mistakes clearly appear in my mind. It seems to me I hear a voice speaking to my mind. "You could have been more useful in the family, in society. You have missed a lot of opportunities." I become my own prosecutor and accuser. I cannot forgive myself for being so passive the last week in the concentration place in Posvol! The days pass. Then weeks.

FIVE.

SLAUGHTER IN THE FOREST

One evening Petronele tells us details of the mass killings. She had heard it from a woman who lives in a house near the forest, the slaughter place.

On the 26th of August, the morning we escaped, buses came to the streets where the Jews were concentrated. In a separate bus the nazis arrived- not only Lithuanians but also Latvians and Ukrainians. Jews were ordered to take small bags of food for one day and quickly get onto the buses. The Nazis' cruelty was astonishing. They kicked and whipped the Jews with lashes, and guns.

In a single file buses reached the forest. The buses, full of Jews packed in like cattle, came to a standstill. Nazis opened the doors. They shouted fiercely, giving orders: "Take off your clothes. Run to the graves, now!" The victims saw the graves. They saw the hundreds of armed murderers. They saw Death.

The Nazis beat the Jews with guns and whips. The Jews ran in all directions but the murderers, like hounds, pursued, chased them. Many Jews in their last revolt jumped on the backs of the Nazis. A few victims in frenzy ran to hide behind the trees, others grasped tree branches and raised them against the murderers. They were all shot.

Some, as if driven completely mad, threw stones. They all met a sudden death.

One woman hid her baby under a tree, covering him with a sweater. Then, pulling out her hair, screaming, she ran into the grave.

The inhuman shout, the cries of women and children did not reach the heavens, The trees bowed down their branches as if calming them down. "We have already seen beasts attack victims in the forest. All people have to die at the end, such are the rules of nature. Sometimes, even the strongest lion has to give in." The muddy boots of murderers kicked in all directions. Their guns fired over the whole span of the grave. In a few minutes the earth was covered with bleeding bodies. The murderers dragged the bodies to the grave. They threw children and babies into the hole as they throw stones, painted red. The first bus was finished. Then the second arrived.

In a few hours three graves were full of trembling bodies. The murderers covered the graves with lye that instantly turned red. For three days and three nights the forest was filled with horrifying sounds. The instinct to live was so great. At night some of the half-dead crawled out of the grave to the bushes. They could not move too far. In the morning the murderers found them and killed them the second time. Nobody escaped from those graves.

The Lithuanian woman who witnessed the slaughter ran away crying hysterically.

The next spring, a new kind of roses grew on the grave. Roses had a special color. They were fed with warm blood.

At Petronele's house, Chaim and I become different human beings, without emotions, without feelings. We do not smile; we do not cry. We talk very little. Every morning we face the mere fact that we must have survived only to wake up one more morning. In the evenings we talk about the past, about the present. We have no future.

Occasionally, a prayer comes to my mind. "If someday life will be normal on earth, let me be able to help other people, let me be wise enough to share all the best I have." Now, I can see the end of the earth.

We spend the days in the tiny room hiding from neighbors; we spend the nights in the cow stable. We sleep on a hay bed.

Six weeks have passed. One day the bad news arrive. A neighbor noticed us and we must leave. It is dangerous for everybody. Cheponis brings worn-out clothes for Chaim; Petronele gives me a patched dress and a scarf. We look like country beggars. The clothes are supposed to hide our Jewish identity.

As Petronele and Elizabeth say goodbye, their eyes are full of tears. They advise us to seek help from poor people. Cheponis advises us to go to rich people.

The two sisters say a short prayer to their God. We are going. We leave them our watches in gratitude.

SIX.

THE WORLD

Cheponis shows us the road leading to my town. "We are going to look for my old neighbors," I say. This is a lie to hide my shame. In reality, we have no place to go. Our neighbors behaved like enemies, they refused to help us, they took our house.

Chaim and I, dressed like beggars, each with a stick in hand, set in the direction of Vabolnik.

We are calm. I am cold to any thought about my death. I hope somebody will help us, but I am not planning whom to ask for help. We do not talk to each other as we take each step along the road that leads to my town.

It is a beautiful day, yet we are beggars, without feelings, without hopes, without fears. The sun is shining the sky is blue. It seems to be very quiet.

Four hours later we find a shelter in a path leading to a little forest. We sit down to rest. We share some food from the straw bag. There is no fear in my heart, no tears.

We rest for about two hours, then we get up to continue our walk. We do not hurry. The road seems to be safe. Many people pass by and do not pay any attention to us. Farmers pass in carts drawn by horses. Nowhere on us is it written that we are Jews.

The evening brings darkness. The houses in the villages are scattered sparsely from one another. Every farmer's house sits in the middle of his plot of land.

We approach people working in the fields or in their yards, Four farmers refuse to give us shelter, even in the stable. The fifth farmer, a very poor one, agrees to allow us to rest on the haystacks in the threshing barn. But first he takes us to the house.

In the living room we see a long table with benches leaning against the walls. A smaller bench is at the other side of the table; a bigger bench along the wail. That is the furniture.

The farmer and his wife are dressed in muddy clothes, with many patches. They have just returned from the fields. The four children are barefoot, in simple trousers. These are the people who would stretch a hand to help a squashed worm.

They serve noodle soup with milk and bread. The parents, the children, Chaim and I enjoy this supper together.

Day and night we spend in the barn. We go to the house only to have our meals. They tell us stories about good Jews and bad Jews. We start getting worried. After three days, the farmer suddenly leaves for town. We leave them in a hurry without saying goodbye.

I feel sorry about leaving without even thanking them, but I am suspicious. Chaim does not trust them either. Their stories frighten us.

We leave the house and again start looking for other people. We see a man and a woman working in a garden, taking in the vegetables. The wife cleans the beet roots and puts them together in a heap. We approach them. I tell my story: "We are Jews from Vabolnik. We escaped from the school. We have stayed with several farmers..." The woman listens carefully. Having heard my name she cuts me short. She knows my parents. Her name is Shimkunas. We are only six miles away from Vabolnik. She was a customer of our small grocery store. She used to buy sugar, herring, and cigarettes. She likes us, "Your father is a good man, he has never cheated us." Her children were friends of my brothers.

We have shelter for two weeks. We are not allowed to go out at all, not even into the yard. I sew, mend, or clean the house. I clean the windows; Chaim washes the floor. I sew; Chaim threads the needles. In the evenings we all talk together. Shimkunas likes us. She condemns her neighbors.

But it is too dangerous to stay in one place. An enemy can see us. The neighbors may suspect us. The Nazis can find us. The neighbor, Barauskas, has a fifteen-year-old son who cooperates with the Nazis.

Two weeks later we leave this place too. The next week we stay at three different farms. The first farmer was a customer at my father's store. He was friendly but could not keep us for more than two days. The second farmer was uneasy. He kept repeating how dangerous it is to house a Jew. We left the next day. The third farmer did not like either Russians or Germans. "The Jews were our neighbors for centuries," he said. He kept us for three days.

Wandering from house to house we run into a young farmer, Vaslavichus. I tell him our story. I tell him how well I can work in the fields. He hesitates but finally agrees.

He leads us to a little barn that has an open window but no door. We get in through the window. He brings straw for us to sleep on, a pillow, a blanket and sheets. He also brings some food and a scarf. He smiles and puts his hand on my shoulder, "Everything will be all right," he assures me. "You will work in the fields, Chaim will work in the barn."

Vaslavichus does not allow Chaim to get out of the barn. It is too dangerous to see a man working in the fields. Nobody suspects me: a woman dressed in muddy working clothes, I look like a young schoolgirl. Many farmers used to go to the town and hire a young girl to help in the house. To bring a man in a house is of much greater significance. A man to help is the symbol of status. The man needs a good salary that only very rich farmers can afford.

Chaim seems nervous. He takes a few bites of food and starts collecting old sacks in a pile.

I swallow the food. Then I put on the scarf. I am ready for fieldwork. In a few minutes the farmer takes me to the field. He explains how to pull the beetroots and leaves. I carefully pull out the beetroots. I use a knife to clean the end part of each beetroot. Two hours later Vaslavichus comes to inspect what I have done. He likes my work. We can stay here, for a while.

The fields have long lines with ripe vegetables: beetroots, cabbage, carrots, and radishes. My work is to tear apart and separate the stem from the root of every single vegetable with a knife. I begin with the beetroots.

I fill up a basket and carry it to a heap in the field. There are many heaps set in a line. Each root must be cleaned. I cut off the leaves and clean the mud from every vegetable. Then I make two heaps: the first out of the leaves and the second out of the roots.

At three-day intervals Vaslavichus comes to take the vegetables to a special barn for storage.

I leave the barn at sunrise, alone. Sitting on the wet earth in the gardens and fields, I have time to think and speak to every blade of grass, to every leaf nearby, to every worm crawling in any direction. They have the right to live and to move and I do not! I can not stop thinking of my dearest, of all my people suffering in the claws of the beasts. I look at the birds who fly in groups every day. I have a vision: the birds come from the slaughterplace, and in their beaks are drops of human blood.

I torture myself with thoughts. I can only find mistakes in my actions with my parents before the war: I accuse myself of having been indifferent to my parents. When I would come for summer vacations with my girl friends, I never had time to spend with my parents.

Why did we leave my parents and run?

In the evenings Chaim and I talk and talk. The barn is our home; the straw is our mattress. Visions fill my mind and yet feelings have left me. I am a stone full of dreams.

I see myself dead in Heaven. Everyone wants to know what happens after death. Now I have the opportunity to think about this.

In Heaven I criticize myself, and think over my life on earth, My parents are near me. I have made so many mistakes. I have not acted, have not resisted in the concentration place in Posvol. We just keep talking and talking.

A ray of moonlight is filtering through the window in the barn. It is quiet all around. Everybody has gone to bed. Only at night Chaim and I feel secure enough to discuss what has happened.

What are the forces that converted young fellows into murderers? Only by being close to each other do we have the strength to calmly talk about this.

My family is probably dead. Chaim's family is probably dead. He says, "We can not change our fate."

Sometimes I remember our life before the war. In the autumn before the war, I bought a present, a woolen sweater, for our maid. Chaim suggested that I give her the present later, when we return from our vacation. I never gave her the gift. I also wanted to buy a hat for my father but could not find the right size. So I postponed buying it to a later date. My father never got the hat.

Oh, if I could only begin my life all over again. I have many plans in my mind. If I could only come to life again. But I feel as though I am sentenced to death. Vaslavichus will not keep us forever. There is no "tomorrow."

On a cold October day, when I finish the fieldwork, Vaslavichus comes and says goodbye. He is afraid to prolong our stay at his house. He mentions a few names of farmers who might help us. He wishes us goodbye.

So, again we are on the road. Maybe we will meet people who will pity us. Pity us? I feel disgusted. I weep with shame as we walk towards Vabolnik.

The streets start to look familiar as we pass by the Synagogue. I realize, we are only three hundred yards from my parents' house, I look around hoping to see a neighbor working in a vegetable garden; hoping to see Shlomo, the milkman, delivering buttermilk; hoping to see men walking to the Synagogue. Four months have passed since we all lived happily together. Now this familiar place has turned to Hell where the law of the jungle presides, where the beasts of prey attack weak animals.

A familiar face walks by. "It's Giedrikas," says Chaim. I know her well, she used to frequent our little grocery store. She recognizes us and whispers, "Come". We follow her. In the house we meet her husband and an adopted, six year old daughter.

The Giedrikas' are both old, over sixty. They make their living from a primitive sawmill. The husband works alone. Farmers who bring beams and girders help him lift the planks. Here, we have no work. We are just hiding from the sight of strangers.

In the house I do various odd jobs: cooking, cleaning, and sewing. Chaim is my help. The door is always locked. When anyone knocks, we do not open it.

One day, somebody knocked violently at the door. We all jumped with fright. The six-year-old girl was confused. She asked in a trembling voice, "Is he a Jew? I am afraid he has come to take me in a sack." I calmed her down. I told her that Jews love little children.

It is the first week of January, 1942. Giedrikas rushes into the house, obviously very upset. She is pale and breathes heavily as if she had seen a vampire. She tells us to hurry and leave the house. A neighbor has warned her that the Nazis are coming to take us.

We must hurry and leave. My shoes are worn out. I put on Chaim's shoes and tie them to my feet with a rope. Giedrikas gives Chaim old rubber galoshes, which must also be tied with a rope, and a hat which may fit a farmboy.

We thank them. Giedrikas suggests that we approach a few farmers who live just outside of Vabolnik.

We decide to leave my native town. The police know about us. One neighbor has betrayed us.

Again we are homeless in the glittering snow, in the cold wind. I am already frozen. The first two farmers we ask for help refuse to give us shelter.

We continue on our way. I cannot walk. Chaim drags me by my hands. I feel as if I am skating. We cannot speak or think. The cold is paralyzing.

Suddenly we see a woman walking in a yard. She carries a pail of water and is about to reach her house. We approach her. We do not know her. Maybe she is an enemy. Maybe her sons are Nazis. Maybe she is a wolf in the shape of a woman.

I do not want to be killed. The desire to live is strong. Chaim talks to the woman. She gets frightened. She orders us to leave.

A few feet away from Chaim I hear the words "Pity us; we are frozen to death." Hearing the word "pity" gives me strength in rage. I come nearer and cannot control my words "You ask the murderer to pity, to give us a shelter," and to her I say, "You, murderer, come and kill both of us. Our blood will fall on the heads of all of you, murderers." Enough, I decide, enough to be so miserable. It is better to die. But how? I do not cry. I pray to God to bring me death. Chaim and I agree to go to the police in my own town and let them kill us. Or maybe the cold will solve the problem.

Chaim drags me. He recognizes the pathway leading to Vaslavichus, the farmer who had kept us for six weeks. Again, the hope to live rises from the ashes.

It is late at night when we near the house of Vaslavichus. Chaim knocks at the door. Vaslavichus himself opens the door. He is sorry but he cannot accept us. He has guests! We turn back toward Giedrikas' where we had left eight hours ago.

We do not speak. I feel my hands. They are freezing, but the pain has left my fingers. My feet do not trouble me anymore, I am a block of ice. Chaim goes ahead. He drags me. I slide. He goes ahead. My mind is strangely full.

In a few hours everything will come to an end! In my mind I am living back the last day in Posvol.

Was it worth to escape and torture myself? Why live if nobody likes me? A voice of anger rises inside me. I have no remedy.

I have not done anything. I have not set houses on fire. I am ice.

Chaim drags me back to the house of Giedrikas. We knock at the door. The woman is frightened. She whispers, "Police is looking for you. They left just a few minutes ago. Go to the cow stable." She hands us a key through the window. A dim light on a pole illuminates the stable window. We come nearer.

A cow stands up as if expecting more food. Two sheep continue sleeping. Chaim gathers some straw in a corner. We lay down.

I am stiff. The pain has disappeared from my feet and fingers. I cannot move. Even my thoughts are frozen. While Chaim sleeps I dream near the cows and lambs.

I begin to think again, but now I am not thinking of heroism.

The dream carries me away to the sun, to the stars and oceans.

There is one God, one world.

In the morning the woman brings us soup and bread. We get back our strength. We do not disclose our plans. We say goodbye. She is indifferent.

We are on the street again. Unable to think of where to go, we decide to go straight to the police. I will only say a few words: "Murderers, here we are. We are still alive." Inside, a voice contradicts me, "Why tease the animal? Do I want more torture before dying?" I will be quiet, close my eyes, hope for pity.

We decide to go straight to the police. Suddenly I stop. I hear a voice inside my heart. "Is it heroic to come close to the wolf and tell him, please, do kill me?" I turn to Chaim. "No, we will not go to the police. If they catch us- this is our fate, but we will not give up."

On the way out of the town we go to the street where only Lithuanians live. It is a very short street parallel to Kupishky Street where my parents lived. Between the two streets are houses and vegetable gardens. I badly want to hear my old Vilkas, a German shepherd, bark, but I do not. I hope Vilkas, our trustworthy friend, has a good shelter with the new owner of our house. Will he get used to the new owners? Will he be a good guard at night?

I am afraid to meet people. The town is so small. Everybody knows each other. We do not look around. I am afraid to show my face. Our beggar clothes are good masks to hide our Jewish faces. We try not to look at each other. We do not speak and only hasten our steps. At last we are out of my native town.

I am afraid to turn, to look back. Still, I turn for a glance and both of us sigh bitterly. We leave my home forever.

Forever! Nobody wants us. Not even my childhood friend Adzia came and offered us shelter. We have been driven out of our houses. Somebody is using our house without being punished. Somebody is using our furniture. It is not a crime to steal property from the Jews.

I can not speak to Chaim. I only bite my lips. I speak to my God. "Why, God? Can people be happy living in the houses of murdered people? Can people be comfortable wearing clothes that were stripped off dead bodies? Can they enjoy the gold chains and rings? What is justice and what is crime in this world?"

I cannot stop, but I turn around to look back once again. Is somebody following us? We are a short distance out of the town. On my right I recognize the house of a farmer to whom my father gave our cow and a few sacks of corn. I decide to enter the house. Chaim agrees. We knock at the door. The wife, Vitkauskas, opens the door.

She jumps, frightened, then recognizes us. I ask for shelter for a few days. She answers in a low voice. She herself is afraid of Germans. She tells us to wait. My fingers are frozen. In a few minutes she brings us back a basket of food. I throw it back and shout, "We will rather die in the cold. How can we remain alive if people close their doors?" We leave.

But the wish to live is so strong. I remember another farmer, further away, again a friend of my father's. My parents have left a few pieces of furniture, several watches, and a sewing machine there. We continue our way through hills of snow and ice. We are frozen. The windstorm pushes me forward. No man, no dog is to be seen in such cold weather.

The snow reaches our knees. For a moment I feel like collapsing on the snow. Chaim prods me: "Sheina, a young fellow is following us. We must go on." Finally we approach the house of the farmer.

The hostess of the house, Ratsinskas, recognizes us. I see tears on her cheeks. She takes us to the second wing of her house, telling us to keep out of the sight of her husband. He is probably a nazi collaborator. She makes us a bed with quilts and pillows. She brings us hot milk and bread. I cannot hold back my tears. I am a beggar at other people's mercy.

For two days we have a warm bed. Later on her brother, who is also a friend of my father's, takes us with him. He is afraid to keep us in his house. At night he shows us a way to an old barn which is used to dry the flax-weed and is always full of smoke. At night we sleep in the drying room.

In the room there is an oven which slowly burns large wet pieces of wood. The smoke from the oven fills up the room and dries the flax weed stacked on the shelves around the wall. This is our shelter. It is too dangerous to keep two Jews in a house, The farmer bears no responsibility for people hiding in the drying room.

In the morning Ratsinskas brings us a warm breakfast. By no means can we stay in her house, but she has plans for us. She introduces us to a boy, Jonas, who is hired to help with the farm work. "Jonas will take you to another farm by horse and buggy," she says. "The farm is in another district, far away from your town, where people will not recognize you."We thank her; however, I am suspicious of Jonas: he is probably a helper of Nazis. But we have no choice.

Jonas takes us twenty miles away to the village of Geleziai. He suggests that we call on the priest. "The priest is a kind man. He might help." Indeed, the priest gives us the names of a few people who might help. Jonas drives us from house to house. We try them all, but not one agrees to give us shelter. They are afraid of Nazis. In the late afternoon we stop at a house of an old woman. She must be in her eighties. She stands at the gates. We tell her, "The priest has suggested that we come to you."

She listens in silence, then finally nods. We may stay. We thank Jonas, and he leaves.

Entering the house we see a young man. We get scared. It seems to me that all young men are murderers. A young girl, Veronika, brings in a bowl of water, soup, and a towel.

The house has no bathroom, no washroom. In the summer they wash outdoors; in winter, they wash at the special corner in the kitchen. Once a week they use a bath house, a sauna filled with hot stones on which they pour water to make steam.

Veronika takes us to another side of the house. We enter a big room, nicely furnished, used only for guests. There are two beds. Veronika brings us a bowl full of water. I begin to wash my face.

The water falling from my face is black, the color of the smoke from the burned wood in the drying room. Nobody had told us that we had black faces. We have no mirror.

I pray to my God for helping the people who are pushed away, the people who have no place in this world. We eat together. We talk.

They do not need my work but I try to sew, to knit, to clean the house, and to wash the linen. The young fellow, Petras, talks with us about Jews, Nazis, and politics. I suspect him of being a helper of the nazis, but I do not care.

One day the old woman, Petras's mother, tells me that Petras is crying at nights. She is not talking very clearly, and I cannot understand everything. "The baby is trembling," she says. He found a half-alive Jewish baby in the forest. The baby was convulsing. I imagine Petras throwing a convulsing baby into a grave. He cannot forget it.

We have our meals at the same table with the whole family. Once we ate an elk. I had the feeling I was eating a living animal. The house is near a forest where the farmers frequently go hunting.

I offer my help as a servant. I begin to train myself in the art of milking a cow. Here there are no machines. Though Veronika helps me, I find it very difficult bending down on my knees, pressing the udders. My fingers are not strong enough to force the flow of milk into a bucket. Still I learn, I milk the cows everyday and in a week I master the job. At my parents' house I was afraid to even get close to a cow. I smile to myself.

SEVEN.

TWO YEARS

One morning, in March 1942, Petras brings me the news: "A rich farmer, Tamulionis, has agreed to take you. He has also agreed to take Chaim but only for one month. It's more dangerous to keep a Jewish man as help."

At night, Chaim and I go to the farmer. He and his family are friendly from the start. They do not ask about my past, they only ask if we are used to physical work since they know we are former teachers.

Before long I master all the jobs in the house, in the stable, and the farmer is pleased. He cannot believe that a small Jewish woman is able to handle farm work.

I get up at four, when it is still dark. First I start a fire in the wood-burning oven, then I chop and prepare the wood for the evening and for the oven. There is no gas, no electricity, so all the cooking is done in this big wood-burning oven.

Next, I clean the pig stable. It has two large sections: one for pigs, another for the pig's food. In the stable stands a big kettle for boiling potatoes and beets. I pour water, start the fire under the kettle, and take two pails to the well. There is a special pail on a long stick attached to a pole that helps lift the water from the well. I pour water into my two pails and carry it with both hands to the stable.

Thirty pails of water are necessary for twenty cows, thirty pigs, and twenty sheep. I must milk sixteen cows. To prepare food for the pigs I mash potatoes in a big bucket, then I add flour, old bread and water. The pigs are fed three times a day.

I prepare breakfast for the family. Every morning, they eat a cabbage soup with bread and peeled potatoes with onions and bacon. Instead of coffee or tea we have a milk soup. For dinner, we prepare the same cabbage soup with bread, meat, pork and sometimes sour milk as desert. In the evenings again milk and bread. We can eat as much bread as we want.

During the meals all the family gathers around the table. A young worker hired for the summer also joins us. The mistress of the house serves the food.

I am very hungry and could swallow an ox but I eat no more than anybody else. I decide in my heart not to eat separately. I could eat the boiled potatoes that were prepared for the pigs, I could drink milk from each cow, but I do not. I feel better being hungry than touching the food that was not given to me.

After breakfast I sew. I sew working clothes, pants and shirts while Chaim patches worn out clothes. I make a few pillowcases. For their daughters, I sew blouses from old dresses.

I also knit. I knit my first dress in two months. Soon, I am able to knit a whole dress in one week. When Tamulionis's wife spins the wool, I help her. I learn to shear the wool from sheep. I wash the wool, dry and ready it for spinning.

Every day I cook, work in the stable, clean the house, and sew. The Tamulionis are pleased. They are even surprised to see the clean floor in the pig stable. The stable floor had been covered with manure, but I cleaned it and I found there were bricks underneath.

A group of ten pigs are enclosed in a cage. To feed them, I put the food in a special barrel. Before giving it to them I take out the leftovers from the first meal. The farmer's wife shows me how. I see the pigs come close to her and lick her hands. But she does not pay any attention. I decide to teach the pigs to obey my commands, to stand aside until I pour in the food.

I succeed in doing it by using a stick. First, I touch them with the stick and tell them in Lithuanian to move away and wait. Then I begin to clean their dishes. If they come too close I move the stick to all sides.

I repeat it several times during the week until the pigs stand far away in the corner, patiently waiting for my permission to eat. I take away the stick. The lesson is over. Even a pig can be taught with the help of a stick.

A pig's life will come to an end. Four times a year, the Tamulionis family kills a pig to increase their meat supply, This is the most difficult day for me. A single bullet kills an animal. The sound of the shot reminds me of the forest, the running, the scared children. Every shot produces the same reaction. I try to hide my tears but the farmer notices them. He laughs at me. He thinks I am sorry for the pig.

I continue to work until the end of May. The farmer needs a shepherd in the summer. I am chosen. At the same time, the farmer thinks, I will be a good help in the garden and in the fields. But what will he tell the neighbors.

Tamulionis tells me his plan: He will take me to the nearest forest early in the morning and leave me there. In the afternoon, he will take me back and pass by the neighboring houses. He will tell them a story that he has taken an orphan to be his shepherdess, My husband, he says, will have to look for another place. Not hesitating for a moment, I refuse the offer. I am not going to stay alone. Chaim and I will leave together.

I have left my parents. I have left my brothers. I am not going to leave my husband. I am a good worker. Tamulionis is not going to dismiss me.

"We will see what we can do," says Tamulionis. Two days later, he notifies me, "We have a shelter for Chaim. Chaim will stay with my brother who lives twelve miles away." Tamulionis is really pleased with me, a maid who works like two. The next morning, Tamulionis takes me to the forest on his way to Ponevezh. Ponevezh is a big town with a market where they sell grain and vegetables.

I am alone in the forest. I wait until evening for Tamulionis to pick me up on his way back from the market.

I feel I have come to another planet. It is five o'clock in the morning. The sunbeams illuminate a large field filled with little bushes. To the right of the field is a big forest of pine trees. I walk around to learn the place. There are many mushrooms and berries. I can easily identify the berries that are poisonous. I am calm.

What a wonderful world has been created for the wild beasts. I am not afraid of the beasts although Tamulionis warned me about the wolves in this forest. Among them I can breathe freely. I am afraid, however, of men.

Seeing a man, I run quickly to the forest to hide behind a thick oak tree. I do not turn back again to look at the forest.

I listen to everything: the singing of birds, the branches falling from a tree. I am frightened by the sound of footsteps.

Late afternoon, Tamulionis is back with a horse and buggy. He takes me home slowly, introducing me to all the neighbors on the way. I am an orphan, not a clever one, and older than an average shepherdess.

Coming to his house, I begin a new life. I do not hide from anybody, but I do not speak to anybody. I continue to do my job. The next week the farmer will train me to take the herd and flock to the fields. I worry I will not be able to hold the cows and sheep in the open fields.

The last evening before the start of the shepherdess job I am scared. What if I do not succeed in holding the animals? Tamulionis promises to help, but my imagination frightens me. I have a sleepless night.

In the morning, I swallow my breakfast and wait. Tamulionis finishes his breakfast and accompanies me to the stable. He ties up the cows. He opens the doors of the stable. I am flushed. The whole multitude- the herd and flock- push each other away. Every cow jumps out on its front feet raising its hind legs high. I am paralyzed with fear. Here is the end of me.

Tamulionis is absolutely calm. In minutes, with a whip he gathers the flock. The flock obeys the whip. He leaves me alone in the field.

An hour is enough for me to become a shepherdess. The cows enjoy themselves eating the fresh grown grass. The sheep do the same. I have a leash in my hand.

I take my knitting. Again I find time to think about all that happened to my people. I try to speak to my cows, to the fields, to the lake nearby. Everything is alive! I listen to the songs of the birds. I watch the frogs in the lake. For the first time I see the real beasts in the fields. In the fields I speak aloud.

I am a backward orphan. Nobody talks to me. I speak to my herd and flock. I do not understand their language. Still, I try to guess their speech by their movements. I watch the sheep and the lambs. A stronger sheep pushes away the weaker lamb that finds a tasty piece of fresh grass. When a lamb sticks his horns against a bigger sheep, I understand. Although the sheep is bigger and stronger, the lamb stands for its rights.

The animals are my friends. I try to share all my problems with them, in particular, with the sheep. The sheep seem to be so obedient.

I try to overcome my tears. I try to smile to the sun that gives me light and warmth. Any day, I think, could be the last one. I can be caught by the murderers.

I decide neither to weep nor to think of death. Among my herd and flock I begin to think of my days at school. I accuse my teachers. They taught me to be religious, to love physical work. Nobody taught me how to protect myself against an attack by a nazi. Why did I not act when I was in Paris Street? I blame myself.

I ask my friends in the fields, "Why does even a little lamb protect itself from a stronger sheep? Why are my unhappy people not able to fight the murderers?"

How to handle a lion? On a sunny day he jumps on the victims. What does one do when the murderers stand nearby with guns? The trees stand still. The clouds hide our God.

In the fields, far away from human beings, I speak to my God whose name I have not found. I am calm by offering my sorrows and my heart to my God. I thank Him for the sunshine, for the birds' songs.

Every morning at sunrise, I leave my straw bed. I thank my God for letting me see another day. Oh God, help me overcome my fear. Help me avoid the disasters of the new day. Sometimes I think the disaster is near. Then, God's voice calms me, "Be happy, it could have been worse."

I can smile. In the presence of the farmer's family, I always smile. I realize how foolish the farmer's daughters are who cry because their clothes are not matching. They are free to dance and sing until late at night. I cannot understand why the daughters are unhappy.

Here, in the fields, I want to find an answer. Chaim is in a safe place. He cannot work in the fields. But Tamulionis promises to take care of him as long as I stay in his house.

On nice summer days the youngest daughter, Adele, substitutes for me in the fields. I am more useful in taking in the hay and grain.

The men cut the corn with a scythe and the women follow them with sheaths. Every woman bends down and gathers the cut rye. The work continues for seven hours.

Then we stack the hay. The sun and wind dry the hay which we have loaded onto big carts. I jump onto the piles of hay with my bare feet to compress it. Then we take the hay to the threshing barn.

I wonder. Years ago I could not believe that I was able to work in the fields as strong women do. Now, I am very proud. I can do anything. In my heart, I want the farmer to believe that a Jew is as able to do physical work as well as a Lithuanian can.

In the vegetable garden I work without the help of machines. Crawling on my knees, I collect potatoes into a little basket and empty the basket into a large sack. Each sack weighs one hundred pounds. I manage to fill two sacks before breakfast.

On rainy days and Sundays I take my herd and flock to the fields. Instead of an umbrella I get a linen sack. I fold it- the tip on the head point. It covers my head and body down to my feet. Rain, as strong as it may be, does not disturb my flock-they eat the wet grass. After filling their stomach, the cows lie on the grass chewing their cud. They lie close together, warming each other with their body heat.

If it rains, I stand under a tree; if it drizzles, I walk and make circles around the herd, sometimes around the flock. My walk forms zigzags as I hasten pace in the rain. I am barefoot. In the evening, when I return my herd to the stable, nobody ask if I was cold or wet. It is natural for a shepherdess to be wet.

I wait to be praised for not complaining, for not being sick. I do not hear anything. Pretty soon I feel like being one of the living creatures in the field.

For two years I live with the Tamulionis. I work from sunrise to sunset. I do not have much time for anything other than thinking. I cannot forget the slaughter of my dear ones.

In the long winter evenings, neighbors visit my farmer. They talk about the Jews of little towns. I sit and knit in the living room. I listen. "Jews are traitors," they say.

I recall this over and over: What evil did we do to the Lithuanians? I knew my parents and brothers, my Jewish neighbors. All of them used to get up early in the morning. They all had an occupation in a little town. We had a vegetable garden.

I remember my mother used to warn me not to go out of town. The Lithuanians might harm me. Why did we not trust each other?

One morning, Tamulionis comes with the bad news: The neighbors suspect me of being a Jewish girl. He is afraid to keep me any longer. His daughter, Adele, will take me to Kupishky where she is studying.

I am quite calm. What else can Tamulionis do? He has prolonged my life for two years. I am accustomed to my new identity. I even have a false passport.

EIGHT.

TEACHING

It is January, 1944. Tamulionis takes Adele and me to Kupishky. The first week I stay in Adele's room. Adele has girl friends who want to study English, German and mathematics. I still remember these subjects. I can teach them. Her friends know me as the Polish girl who is hiding from the Germans. To be Polish is not as dangerous as to be Jewish.

To find my own room is a big problem. I apply for help to Kupsta, the priest of Kupishky. He is a kind man and finds me a room at once.

Chaim is in another place now. After I left Tamulionis, Chaim had to leave Tamulionis' brother. The same priest, Kupsta, who helped me find a room, found Mantrimas, a new farmer for Chaim. He is only eight miles away. We will be able to see each other more often!

I hope to earn some money from private lessons. Adele gets me ten pupils from different grades. For eight of them, my fee is food. Only two girls can pay me with money and I use it to pay for the room.

I have my students from early morning until late at night. I have no time to think. I do not care whether the neighbors know my identity or not.

Only lonely women live in my neighborhood. In the evenings I see them sitting near their houses. I talk to them. They do not ask questions.

Tomorrow does not exist for me. If I have enough food, I share it with my neighbors. I thank my God for allowing me to help needy people.

In the spring of 1944, we notice a change in the political situation.

The Germans start recruiting young Lithuanian boys and girls to the German factories. The German soldier's retreat and the young Lithuanians hide from the Germans.

One morning two German soldiers come near our house. An old woman, one of my neighbors, runs into my room with the warning. Two Lithuanian girls and I run to the yard where we take shelter in the outhouse. The German soldiers find the two girls but they do not find me. They had opened all doors, except mine. A miracle?

I continue my work. I like my students; they like me.

The students bring in the rumors that the Germans are losing. I want to believe the news. But I am afraid. I try not to think about it.

On Sundays Chaim and I meet and we talk about the hope that we will survive. In my heart, where there should be joy, there is sadness. I do not feel like being a wife. I have lost interest in private life. I will never be like I was before the war.

July, 1944. The school year is coming to an end. Where will I go now? After the war, I want to see the world. Maybe I will meet somebody from my family.

One morning, the mother of one of my students, Vaitiekunas, says, "We need a teacher for the whole summer for my two sons in the village ten miles away. Please let me know in a few days if you can do it." I do not want to look desperate. This is from heaven. My answer is clear. I do not have any doubt.

In a few days Vaitiekunas comes back. "I accept your offer," I say. "What about the pay?" she asks. I try to ignore the question. Still, she insists, "What about the pay?"-"A winter coat," I answer. We make a deal and she takes me to her house.

In the house she shows me to a room and leaves me alone to rest. I fall on my bed and burst into tears. I am lonely without my parents, without my friends. I do not try to stop my tears. I do not hide my face in the pillow. "Why?" I ask my God.

"Why is it that I cannot thank you?"

In the morning, after breakfast, we begin our work. The three sons of Vaitiekunas are my pupils. We have a separate room which has a long table with a few chairs and a sofa against the wall. This is our classroom.

We study for about five hours. If we have time left, we take long walks around the farm. Sometimes, we go to the fields to help with the work.

Being a teacher I find myself with free time. Occasionally I help the maid. I compare her work with mine at Tamulionis. There I worked like two maids.

If this is so, why do the Lithuanians say that Jews do not know how to work? They do not know us. How can I have really trusted them? Only now my eyes have opened. Lithuanians are work loving, honest people- but their education is wrong, their whole culture is wrong.

I hear rumors in the village that the war is nearing the end. As the Russian Army advances to the borders, the Jewish soldiers are going to take their revenge on the Nazis. I try to hide my feelings. I am happy about the German defeat but I am also afraid. Maybe the Russians will not take over so quickly. I do not know how to behave with the Russians.

One night Vaitiekunas wakes me up. She wants me to be with her. She has seen Russian soldiers.

I hurry to the yard with her. We see many soldiers marching on foot. Some of them enter our yard and ask for bread. I slice the bread and give a piece to each soldier.

I cannot believe my eyes. I am helping hungry soldiers.

Where are the Germans? Has the war really ended? I have no newspapers, no radio. I do not know what to think. Three days later, Chaim arrives.

"The Russians are here," he says. "We are free!" We embrace and weep.

Chaim tells me his adventures while coming here on foot. "The Russian soldiers stopped me. They asked me my name and occupation."

Now, I have to present Chaim to Vaitiekunas. They do not know my identity. They do not know that I am married.

Chaim visits me every Sunday. We cannot get used to the thought that the Germans have left. We talk about our obligation to join the Russian Army and fight the Nazis. Chaim has no obligations to his farmer. He decides to go to Ponevezh, a big town.

In Ponevezh, Chaim meets Jewish soldiers and a few single Jews who have survived. Maybe somebody from my family is still alive. It is too early to look for them. The Germans are still around. Chaim goes to Ponevezh for the second time.

Two weeks later I receive a postcard from him. He is in the Russian Army. He tells me to continue my work and wait for further notice from him.

I have to get used to the new situation. Do I believe in the Russian Law? Do I believe in their slogans, that nobody will kill me because I am Jewish? I feel miserable. I am a tiny dot, too small to change anything.

I fulfill my everyday duties, teaching the children. Soon, they pass their exams and I am free, free to be homeless.

Return to the slaughter place in the forest with survivors, 1947.

Teaching in Lithuanian School, Kaunas, 1956.

With Petronele, who saved us, with the family in Vabolnik, 1956.

In front of Petronele's house that served as our shelter during the War.

Visit to the monument erected to commemorate the victims of the War, 1962.

Another visit to the monument with survivors and the children of survivors in 1965.

*Children of survivors in the reunion of the last Jewish Grade
School in Kovno, the picture taken in Israel, 1975.*

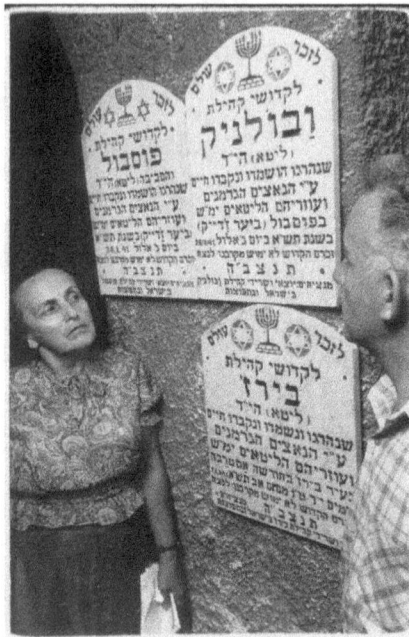

*Memorial for the victims of Vabolnik, Yad Vashem, Israel,
1979.*

NINE.

LIBERATION

I
t is September, 1944. Again I decide to go to the priest Kupsta. He advises me to see the same farmer, Mantrimas, who has sheltered Chaim. He gives me a letter of recommendation. Vaitiekunas agrees to take me on his cart drawn by hors

We say goodbye. Vaitiekunas promises to keep in touch. And, as soon as the dressmaker comes to their house, he will come and get me for a few days until the dressmaker makes my winter coat - my summer's pay.

Mantrimas accepts me. I openly tell him: "I am waiting for a letter from Chaim. I might leave unexpectedly." Still, the family strongly wants me to teach their children. They even agree to take me to Vabolnik.

On the way to Vabolnik, I actually feel my heart pounding with hope. Maybe my brother is alive, maybe my mother. I have no hope of finding my sick father alive.

After a two-hour trip, we arrive in Vabolnik. We stop right in front of my house. I try not to cry. I feel as if my heart is ready to explode.

The house is in the same spot. Now the Lithuanian dwellers are inside. Everything is in its place as if nothing has happened during these three years. I cannot find our dog. The woman tells me he is in the country with her relatives.

Maybe our cow. I do not care. None of my family, none of my Jewish neighbors are alive. Who gave me the right to survive? How will I live among the people who hate me?

"The Vainer brothers are alive," says the woman, and gives me their address. I leave with Mantrimas quickly to see them.

Yacov, the younger brother, runs out of the house to meet me, tears on his cheeks. We embrace and cannot stop weeping. We cannot begin talking. Then comes his brother, Shlomo. The same cries. We talk. The Vainers had escaped that morning when we were all gathered in the Synagogue. They suspected the slaughter but could not really believe it would happen. All their relatives were killed.

Shlomo and I walk along the streets of our native town. We stop near every Jewish house. This one was a good gardener; that one was a good shopkeeper; that woman used to bake the best white bread; there lived a watchmaker; here lived a shoemaker; there was the club of the Jewish youth organization which had parties once a week. The houses stand in the same places. We see no people in the houses. Maybe they are ashamed to look into our eyes.

Vainers and I have so much to say, but my farmer is in a hurry. We embrace like a real brother and sister.

I depart from Vabolnik, the little town where my parents and close relatives lived for more than fifty years. I return with Mantrimas.

For the third time, I begin a new life. Now everybody knows that I am Jewish. I am not afraid to walk around the village. I even get friendly with another teacher. In the evenings, we study Russian together.

Everything changes quickly. Only a few months pass and what a revolution. The Germans are defeated. The Russians are here. The local population takes orders from the new government.

I get busier. The mornings I spend with the Mantrimas children; the afternoons I teach a neighbor's daughter. Days and weeks pass.

I am on the earth again, in a New World where I am the only Jew in the village.

At the end of March I receive a letter from Chaim. His regiment is in Kovno, the capital of Lithuania. He found out about his cousin who lives in Kovno. He tells me to go there and live with his cousin. I prepare for my departure.

I ask Mantrimas to take me back to Vaitiekunas who has promised me a winter coat. He does it willingly. I say goodbye to everyone in the house where I live. I say goodbye to the neighbors.

In two days the dressmaker finishes my coat and Vaitiekunas arranges a ride for me to Ponevezh on a truck that carries construction materials.

Arriving in Ponevezh, I remember my six years here two in a religious school and four in the Hebrew High School. I go to see my old school. I find the house where I rented a room. The houses are firmly in their places.

I take a train to Kovno. I am nervous. There are only Russians and Lithuanians. Nobody is Jewish, not like before the war. I have a feeling I have been sleeping for seventy years. A new generation of people- I know nobody; nobody knows me. On the train, life goes on as before. Only none of my people is riding the train.

When I get off, I look at all the passengers. I see only one dark-haired soldier. I wonder if he is Jewish.

I am afraid. From the train station I walk along Vytautas Street. I am scared to turn back. I have the feeling somebody is following me. I hurry through the streets. At last I find the house of Chaim's cousin. Inside I meet the cousin's wife, Fanny.

A hysterical cry is her first greeting. I cannot stop asking the question: Am I dreaming?

We sit down at the table and have a glass of tea. I ask Fanny many questions: Who of our family has survived? Who else? She tells me that only a thousand Jews have returned from the death camps. Many others went straight to Israel or other countries.

The Synagogue was the place to go, she said. On the bulletin board was a list of survivors. There was also a committee which helped the Jews leave Russia for Israel. Fanny allows me to stay with her until Chaim comes back from the army. It is 1945.

I go out into the streets. I stop people and ask them if they are Jewish. I cannot hold my tears. They comfort me. We must look for a piece of bread. We must look for ways to leave this land of horrors.

Some ways are very risky. A group of Jews try to bribe a Soviet pilot who promises to take them to a European country. He asks for a large sum of money. He takes the money, makes a circle and brings all of them to a police station. Now the immigration gates are closed completely. Nobody can leave Russia.

I go to the Synagogue and talk to people. Every day people are coming from death camps. I do not know them, still we kiss and embrace.

Always the same questions: How did you survive? How can we leave for Israel?

I walk along the streets of Kovno, the town I knew before the war. I know every place where Jewish people lived. I know the shops. The buildings remind me of the people who have been murdered for the crime of being Jewish. The buildings have changed. They are darker as if mourning the death of their first dwellers.

I visit the house which has been the Jewish Cultural Center. There is no sign of Jewish life. The building has been converted into a warehouse.

TEN.

THE LAST JEWISH SCHOOL

It is April, 1945. I come to a school where at last I see Jewish children. I stop near the gate to watch them play in the yard. Where have they come from? Was it the American army that liberated them?

On the ground floor I see a kitchen, a large room. Three women are busy cooking. I ask them where I can find the director of the school. They coldly point me to the first floor.

I greet the director who tells me they are in need of a primary school teacher. He speaks in short sentences. I want to ask him where he had been hiding during the war, but instead I simply ask where to apply for a teaching position. He advises me on how to regain my certificate of education and I resume my work on May 2, 1945.

Chaim is transferred to Kovno, a new place for his regiment.

We can see each other at least twice a week. We talk about the Jewish School, about our new life. We have no money except the income from my first job.

During the summer vacation, the director of the school leaves for Israel. The Jewish community is worried. As if by miracle Chaim leaves the army and becomes the director of the Jewish School.

Sheina Sachar-Gertner

He organizes and shapes it into a regular school: all new students are registered, classes are scheduled as any other school. There are more than one hundred children. The school is both a Jewish center and a regular school. While it appears to be no different from any other school in the area, it is the main Jewish center.

All the subjects are taught in Yiddish because there is a mixture of languages here: some of the pupils speak Lithuanian; the children who have returned from Siberia, speak Russian.

I watch the children, their innocent eyes, which radiate when they solve a problem. I cannot hold back my tears. How could someone kill children. Did he not think of the day when he, the murderer will have children? What evil power makes someone kill children?

I remember in the years before the war, there was great hatred between the Lithuanians and the Germans. The Lithuanians believed the town of Memel belonged to them; the Germans believed it to be theirs. I saw the Germans throw telescopes and books out of the Lithuanian Institute. It was 1938. Three years later some Lithuanians became Nazis. They killed children. How did their educators and parents make such a mistake? How could they bring up murderers?

I remember the war. "Why have I not gone to see the graves where my parents and brothers are buried? None of the survivors yet dared to see the graves. I must see the graves." I rent a car with the Vainer brothers and we leave Kaunas for Posvol.

The driver stops the car. The graves are just behind the trees. The branches keep nodding, shaking their heads as if asking: "Are you Jewish?" Long branches lean to the ground, showing us the place of the slaughter.

We walk among the trees. Nobody utters a sound, and I hear a loud weeping. We do not look at each other. We look at the grass but we cannot find any marks of the graves. Suddenly I hear the trees: "Look at the flat surface where the trees were cut off."

Vainer is the first one to find two skulls and a few scattered bones. "Maybe these are the remains of the two families-

Kershon and Traub who were the last to remain alive in Posvol," says Vainer. "But maybe not," interrupts Moroz. "I heard rumors that young men at night search for treasures here."

We gather bones and skulls in one pile. I feel like I am holding the skull of my brother. Now I understand the word "remains"- remains of a dead body, left by the birds which swallow flesh.

I find a long naked branch and stick it deep into the ground. I search for the real contour of the grave. There is a pile of bones. The trees keep nodding their heads to the sun. I understand their speech: "God in heaven kept quiet while the cries of mothers frightened the worms and snakes. The clouds pass by quickly as if frightened by the distant echo of the bullets. Only the sun shows its generosity- the bright light has closed the eyes of the children."

We bury the bones under the grass and cover them with the earth soaked in blood.

Vainer says Kadish. I murmur my own prayer for my parents, for my brothers, and for my friends. I am guilty. I do not even know when their hearts stopped.

Vainer finishes the Kadish. I finish my prayers. I feel as though I am at a funeral. It occurs to me that we should build a monument, a symbol to the native people that not everybody was killed, that nobody has been forgotten.

We turn back. I glance at the trees which wave me goodbye. We walk in silence watching the grass as if searching for more remains.

I keep repeating to myself: "Murderers. Why? How could you kill the children?"

In 1950, before the end of the school year, the Board of Education decides to close the Jewish School. Jewish books are not published any more.

The Jewish population is against it, but nobody can help. It is the decision of the government. The students are ordered to enter Russian or Lithuanian schools.

Chaim and I are appointed teachers in the Lithuanian School Nr.4, in Kovno. I teach English, Chaim mathematics. In the Lithuanian School we feel quite good. We are not communists but we are sure of tomorrow. Nobody would ever dismiss us because we are Jews.

We persist in trying to emigrate to Israel. We try to get Polish citizenship papers, we have no luck. We try to bribe some officials but we lose the money. Years pass.

Everything goes on. Every year we come to the graves. I have no other place to visit my parents and relatives. I take my children to the slaughter place when the youngest is six. They begin to understand the meaning of these visits. Any time we find any remains we gather them in one place. My children do the same. Nobody has to instruct them.

On the last Sunday of each August, former inhabitants of Birzh join us in our forest. We join them in theirs. The common tragedy in the little towns unites us. Others read Kadish; I say my own prayer, to my own God.

Contrary to the Jewish tradition we bring flowers. I ask myself,

"Did I bring enough flowers to my parents when they were alive?" Who needs them now, the flowers, my prayers, the Kadish from the Sidur?

During those Sundays I visit the farmers who helped me. They become my relatives. I write them letters and send gifts.

I want to build a monument at the slaughter place. We have to get permission from the local municipality in Posvol, from the capital of Lithuania in Vilnius, and even from the capital of Russia, Moscow. After ten years of struggle, we receive the permission.

The opening of the monument is a show where the politicians deliver speeches. We walk to the second monument fifty yards away. I feel I am participating in a real funeral.

We return home exhausted but satisfied. At last I sit down and write a letter to my dead parents! "I have not forgotten you, my dears. I shall never forget you. Now we have a monument. Still, I am guilty for escaping, my dear mother and father. There are no excuses for leaving you among the beasts armed with guns, sticks, and whips. I don't even know when your hearts stopped. I pray in my heart to God to punish me."

ELEVEN.

THE NEW HOMELAND

It is 1965, in Moscow. I never forget that I was saved by the Soviet Army. But we yearn to have a tiny land, our own land. We come to Moscow to watch the Israeli film "Yizkor". Many of the Jews spend their last savings to go to Moscow only to see this film.

During the show I cry. The entire Jewish history is running before me. I see the bitter end of my people in Europe. I see the "halutsim" on their way to Israel. I see my homeland, a land like any other: people studying, working, being creative. I am convinced. The Nazis have not destroyed us.

We live our life around Israel: At home we celebrate all the festivals. We find someone to teach Hebrew to our sons. We listen to the radio news from Israel with the doors closed.

In 1967, the Six-Day War breaks out. We live under great tension. We cannot imagine Israel being able to defeat the enemy.

Day and night we listen to the Israeli radio. We are depressed, We cannot do anything. Our hearts and thoughts are with our soldiers who are defending our tiny land. Suddenly the news arrive- Israel has won the war. We run to see our friends. We embrace and kiss each other with tears in our eyes. We ask each other whether it is real, the Israeli army defeating its enemies. I believe it is from Heaven.

Even Lithuanian people are happy along with us. They stop us in the streets, shake our hands.

We still keep trying to emigrate to Israel. When I visit my friend in Vilna, I hear about a group of thirty Jews who went to Moscow and applied to the Ministry of Internal Affairs for permission. All of them got permissions.

Now I have more courage. I begin to speak openly about my wish to emigrate. A few years ago, I would have been imprisoned.

Twice a month I go to Vilna to inquire about my immigration status. I find a group of people organizing a trip to Moscow to apply to the central authorities. My decision is to join them. This is very dangerous. This is an organized action that could be severely punished by the state.

March 8, 1970. I take a few "sick days" and prepare for the trip to Moscow. I pack warm underwear and some medicine. I am ready for any hardship. I tell a lie to my family: "I am going to visit my friend in Vilna."

In the train station I meet two other women. We are going to Moscow to fight together. We prepare a list of people who want to emigrate. I am not afraid to write down my name and the names of all the members of my family. Everyone must tell the reasons for his wish to leave Russia. I simply write the truth: I would like to live together with my relatives in our homeland. I have no fear.

The next day we come back to wait for our turn. Somebody notifies us to go to the Kremlin. On arrival we see a crowd of young people waiting in the hall.

Two of the leaders have a declaration in their hands. We must sign it. It states: "We demand the permission to emigrate to Israel." When nobody comes out, we prepare for a hunger strike.

About one hundred and eighty of us, mostly young people, take a seat in the hall. We sit and talk in low voices. The doors open and close, people come in and out. They are not Jews. Nobody talks to them.

Five hours later two Russian officers walk in. They talk about our Russian heritage and ask us to leave the room. We refuse. We demand to see the Minister of Internal Affairs instead.

It is March 8, 1970, the evening of Purim. It is getting dark. There are no lights. Suddenly a man gets up. He holds a book in his hand and goes over to the window. The man speaks in Russian. He congratulates us on the evening of Purim. We all answer "Amen". I laugh. On Purim you are supposed to thank God and not say "Amen". I am afraid. Never before in the Soviet Union has anybody dared to say prayers in public.

Even though it is Purim, he begins to read from the "Pessah Hagada". He speaks of our sufferings in Egypt, of Hamman wanting to destroy us. We listen. We understand.

An hour later, the corridors fill up with soldiers. It feels as if we are once again under German occupation. Soldiers with guns walk into the hall. They stand close to the two walls, crowding us against the remaining walls. The first officer introduces himself as the colonel of the city of Moscow. The second officer is the representative of the Ministry of Internal Affairs. The third one is the representative of the police department.

The colonel warns us to leave the hall or they will take more serious action. They give us five minutes to decide. Three minutes pass. We stand up and follow one of our organizers out. Outside the Kremlin in the street we are greeted by the Jewish people of Moscow. In the excitement, we go to the Post Office and send a telegram to Mr. Brezhnev.

In the morning of March 9th, we all meet at the Ministry of Internal Affairs. We see six buses, a dozen cars, many armed soldiers. I feel like in 1942.

Minister Sokolov comes out.He apologizes that he could not come yesterday. I am shocked- a Russian official apologizing to a group of Jews! Sokolov speaks politely about the equality we, the Jews, can enjoy in Russia, on all the achievements of our youth. He speaks of our homeland, Russia. We raise our voices: "No, our homeland is Israel." He speaks of all the money the government has spent to prepare Jewish doctors, engineers and teachers. We reply: "We are ready to pay back."

Sokolov asks, "Why do you want to emigrate to Israel?" An old man answers, "I do not want my children to see bloodshed here in exile." One young woman tells of the brutality in Riga. Sokolov answers by praising her beauty. The women replies: "In Israel I would be even more beautiful."

We talk back and forth for two hours. Finally, Minister Sokolov says: "We will discuss it in the department. In the meantime, go to the secretary and register your names and addresses." We obey. In a month, the permission is granted.

TWELVE.

RETURN

This is my twentieth and last visit to the graves. We are all leaving for Israel. I feel like standing in the midst of dried flesh, bones, and sand. I see the two monuments, which took so much time to be built. Now the inscription on the monuments seems to be strange: "In this place lie five thousand inhabitants of the Soviet Union killed during World War II." The municipality did not agree to the word "Jew". Will anybody ever believe us that in this place people have been murdered only for being Jewish?

I take with me a handful of earth, the soil of the grave. I will bring it to Israel. This was the wish of the victims. I will hand over the bowl with the ashes to Yad Vashem.

I say my own prayers. It is strange. For the third time we participate in the funeral for the same people. Ordinary people have only one funeral.

The day comes to say goodbye to our neighbors. It is not easy. We have many good friends among the teachers. At the same time I cannot forget the great evil that some Lithuanian people had done. They helped the Nazis to kill. I cannot find an answer. What was the power of evil that converted normal people into beasts of the jungle? I cannot forgive. I cannot forget. All I can do is hope.

On the E1-AI plane everyone speaks Hebrew. Some of us shout "Hurrah, Heydad." Tears are in my eyes. I am holding two red tulips that I will give the first Jew who meets me in Israel.

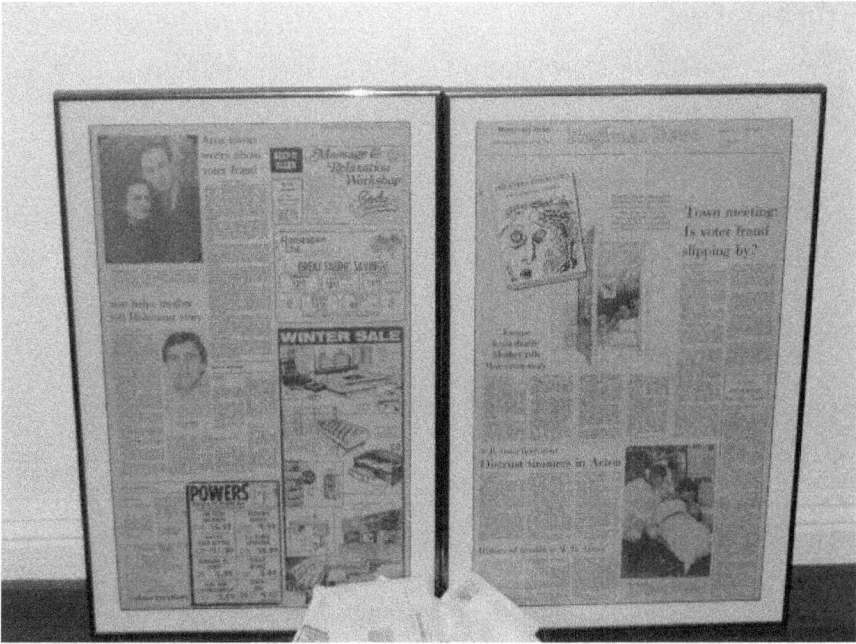

Middlesex News article, Son helps mother tell Holocaust story.

EPILOGUE:

*THE STORY OF THE BOOK - Son helps mother tell Holocaust
story*

*MIDDLESEX NEWS
SUNDAY, JANUARY 30, 1983*

Escape from death: Mother tells Holocaust Story
By Tom Zuppa
News Staff writer

Sheina Sachar-Gertner and her husband, Chaim, are forced
to dodge bullets, hide in goat shacks, take handouts and shelter
from those who dare hide Jews from the Nazis. The fugitive
couple is seeking freedom. Even Sheina's naitive Vabolnik is
unsafe. The police know they are Jews.

They never see a German, nor a concentration camp. They
survive, but the scars remain. Years later, Sheina Sachar-Gertner,
whose son lives in Framingham, lectures on fear and the
Holocaust. She cries as she prepares each lecture.

"I want you to write a book about it." Ilya Gertner tells his
mother, hoping it will stop his mother's tears." I will publish it
for you."

Two and a half years later, Ilya Gertner created Holocaust
Survivors Publishing Company- a labor of love designed solely
to publish his mother's work. Working out of his Bryant Road
home, Gertner made arrangements for his mother's book, "The
Trees Stood Still" to be published in October.

"I just didn't want her to cry," he said. "I-wanted her to get
over it once and for all. I encouraged her to write what happened,
what she felt."

The' book is written from the heart. Death is capitalized,
nazis lower case. "In my heart, I believe he is a nazi," Sheina
writes of one Lithuanian she and her husband met. "Chaim agrees

73

with me. Nothing around me touches my heart. We are in the hands of blind faith."

Later, she writes of Vabolnik; "I am afraid to meet people. The town is so small. Everybody knows each other. We do not look around. I am afraid to show my face. Our beggar clothes are good masks to hide our Jewish faces."

"... We leave home forever. Forever! Nobody wants us. Not even my childhood friend Adzia came and offered us shelter," she writes.

Gertner was not alive during the events of the book, but he is drawn to the story. Except for his parents and a few distant relatives in South Africa, his family was wiped out by the Holocaust.

"It gets me inside," he said. "I cannot go calmly through a few chapters. You wonder how it could happen."

It has also brought back memories. When he was young, Sheina took him to visit the families that gave her shelter, people she called her "new family." She also took him to the makeshift graveyard where many Lithuanian Jews were buried.

"It was like going to a funeral for my grandparents," he said. "A strange funeral every year."

The Gertners left the Soviet Union for Israel in 1972, where Sheina lives today.. Ilya Gertner completed his graduate studies in New York. He moved to Framingham in 1980. about the time he encouraged his mother to write.

It took her "many months" to write an original, longhand manuscript. Gertner turned. a typewritten version over to professional editors, who returned the original back to him with "50 or 60" questions. Most had to do with amplifying stories or making them clearer, he said.

With her son continuously encouraging her, Sheina spent three months on a revised manuscript, which he says passed muster with flying colors. All in all, 2 1/2 years from idea to book.

Gertner says, however, that the book leads people to believe he runs a large publishing house. They send poems and writings on the Holocaust.

He says he has not even committed to publishing his mother's next work, interviews with other Holocaust survivors.

The first book was done for love, not money, Ilya's wife, Rozita, quickly adds.

"The purpose was to disseminate information," she said. "We didn't do this commercially, just to make a profit. It's a type of book people need."

The couple has distributed 100 of the first printing of 500, with universities here and in Israel expressing interest, they said.

Because there is almost no bloodshed in the book, some parents are using the books as their children's non-violent introduction to one of the most violent events in world history, Gertner said.

If they sell all 500, "we'll come close to breaking even, "Mrs. Gertner said, but that's not a concern. "Our people are becoming old," Gertner said. "They have a store to tell. If we don't do something, the world will forget."

THE TREES STOOD STILL

Sheina Sachar-Gertner

SHEINA SACHAR-CERTNER was born in Vabolnik, a small town in Lithuania and now lives in Israel. Today all her free time is dedicated to Holocaust studies.

THE TREES STOOD STILL is the memoir of a young woman who escaped the Nazis by hiding in the forests of Lithuania. Hers is the story of escape - of peasants and barns, a woman of culture, newly married, a teacher - cast into a world of terror, hunger and brutality.

In the "The Trees Stood Still" Sheina Sachar Gertner refers to herself as "a living grave". She tells her story as if it were a prayer: terse, powerful in its simplicity:

> *"I could swallow an ox but I eat no more than anybody else. I could eat the boiled potatoes that were prepared for the pigs. I could drink the milk from each cow. I do not, I am more satisfied by being hungry than touching the food that was not given for me. "*

She and her husband, Chaim, escape to Posvol, her hometown. It is 11 o'clock at night and snowing:

> *"We do not speak. My feet do not trouble me anymore. The pain has left my fingers. Chaim drags me. I slide. He goes ahead. ... Why live if nobody likes rne? A voice of anger rises inside me. I have no remedy. I have not done anything. I have not put houses on fire. I am ice."*

In her journal, she remembers her escape, farm upon farm, indignity upon indignity, until she happens upon a schoolroom and becomes a teacher again. The war ends. She leaves for the Kremlin in search of her final exit visa to Israel.

77

"On the El-Al plane everyone speaks Hebrew. Some of us shout `Hurrah, Heydad'. Tears are in my eyes. I am holding two red tulips that I will give the first Jew who meets me in Israel. "

The book is worthy of yours and the world's attention. In a time when some scholars are suggesting that the holocaust never happened, this manuscript, with its insistent and touching honesty, is a testament to the truth.

READER REVIEWS

Unlike the stories of children who survived the war by hiding among the peasants, *The Trees Stood Still* reveals the experiences of a sensitive, insightful woman. Sheina Sachar-Gertner distills her thoughts and feelings in a compellingly personal, courageous and moving book. Its terse, compressed style evokes the sense of a confessional. What emerges, despite the pain, is an affirmation of mankind's humanity from an individual who is strongly committed to life at the same time that she is forever attached to the souls of the dead. At the end of the book, Sheina, finally granted her emigration papers by the Russians, and she is on the plane headed toward Israel. Clutching two-red-tulips in her hand, she thinks, "I cannot forget. All I can do is hope." Though it was not written with this intent, *The Trees Stood Still*, because of its positive outlook and because it is sparing and understated in its description of violence, could serve as an introductory reading about the Holocaust for adolescents. Its delineations of the complexities and questions inherent in the afterlife of survivors is also most valuable in this regard.

-- M. Budzynski

In the tradition of Eli Weisel's *Night* and Jan T. Gross's *The Neighbors*, Sheina Sachar Gertner tells her story of neighbor turning against neighbor and of her escape from the Nazi occupation of her small town of Vabolnik, Lithuania in 1941.

From the point-of-view of an educated woman, a teacher, with an eye for significant facts, she details the situation that found her hiding in the woods, in barns to the thatched-roofs of two very poor "Christian" sisters, who took her in. After four years of wandering, Sheina rejoins her husband in Kovno, the capital of Lithuania, where 96% of the Jewry where murdered. The few returning from death camps all asked the same question: "How did you Survive?"

To read her book is a lesson in survival for any young woman caught in the turmoil of a world turned upside down. Or, in her own words, "murdered for the crime of being Jewish." And upon seeing what remained of her last Jewish school, she asks, "What evil power makes people kill children?" Written with the cautious clarity of a teacher, her book serves as a non-violent introduction to one of the most violent periods in world history - a must read by all survivors.

-- N. Sachar

The Trees Stood Still reveals the experiences of a sensitive, insightful woman. Sheina Sachar-Gertner distills her thoughts and feelings in a compellingly personal, courageous and moving book. Its terse, compressed style evokes the sense of a confessional. What emerges, despite the pain, is an affirmation of mankind's humanity from an individual who is strongly committed to life at the same time that she is forever attached to the souls of the dead. Though it was not written with this intent, *The Trees Stood Still*, because of its positive outlook and because it is sparing and understated in its description of violence, could serve as an introductory reading to the Holocaust for adolescents.

-- B. Shusterman

As a grade school/junior high librarian I regard this book as a new source of information to both children and parents as to a different experience of the Holocaust. Many parents do not want their young children to be subjected to horror stories describing this period. Ms. Sachar Gertner has managed in an easy and comprehensible way to describe the Holocaust in the way which will not give the children nightmares but at the same time will let them understand what a dark and horrible period it was in human history. I highly recommend this book to 8-12 year olds and to adults of all ages.

-- M. Goldvaser